D1545483

Woolley   History Unearthed

THIS SURVEY OF eighteen archaeological sites
throughout the world chosen to show how the scientific
methods of modern field archaeology have added
to our knowledge of the past has been one of the late
Sir Leonard Woolley's most popular books.
Unfortunately the original edition did not do full justice
to the illustrations. Those in this new version are
printed by photogravure of particularly fine quality.
They are the same as those used in the American,
French, German, Hindi and Swedish editions.

'No better authority than Sir Leonard Woolley could
have been found to write this outstanding account
of the 18 most important archaeological discoveries of
recent times . . . Should be compulsory reading
for everyone interested in archaeology.

Teacher's World

'. . . for those who wish to read the words are drops of gold.'

Times Literary Supplement

History Unearthed

Sir Leonard Woolley

1963 · Ernest Benn Limited · London

OTHER BOOKS ON ARCHAEOLOGY

Digging up the Past   SIR LEONARD WOOLLEY

Archaeology in the Holy Land   KATHLEEN KENYON

Digging up Jericho   KATHLEEN KENYON

MEMOIRS

Sometimes a Soldier   THE REV. G. H. WOOLLEY, v.c.

Gertrude Bell: ELIZABETH BURGOYNE
From Her Personal Papers
Vol I 1889–1914
Vol II 1914–1926

913
W913w
140249

Published by Ernest Benn Limited 1963
Bouverie House · Fleet Street · London EC4

All rights reserved
© Ernest Benn Limited 1958

Printed in Germany by DuMont Schauberg Köln

Contents

Introduction

This volume, a picture-book with its text reduced to a minimum, was designed to deal with the eighteen archaeological excavations in all parts of the world which had made the most important contributions to our knowledge of ancient history, and to emphasize the extent to which such contributions were due to the scientific methods of modern field work. During the last century, when the art of scientific excavation developed, an enormous amount of work had been done, and I was limited to eighteen sites only; it was therefore a matter of rather ruthless selection. I drew up a long list of important discoveries, and almost at once realized that they by no means always fulfilled the two conditions laid down; some which had undoubtedly contributed a great deal to history were not distinguished by scientific method; many sites which had been excavated scientifically had produced results that filled up gaps in our knowledge of history but were not in themselves of outstanding importance. Some things had to be ruled out altogether. The Dead Sea scrolls are of absorbing interest, but they have nothing to do with the story of excavation; like the equally important Tell el Amarna letters they were found, accidentally, by peasants, and hawked about on the antiquities market until their value was recognized and they found a purchaser. Reluctantly I ruled out the cave paintings of southern France and Spain, because their discovery involved no archaeological work in the strict sense of the word, and, again with reluctance, the unearthing of Pompei which has been going on for a century and a half, beginning with some desultory "collecting" of antiques under the Bourbons and continuing down to the present day, when meticulous method recalls the past to life instead of merely adding to museum collections.

On the other hand I could not omit the discoveries made by Layard in Mesopotamia and by Schliemann in Mycenae and Troy. They, of course, worked in the old days before General Pitt-Rivers by his excavations in Wessex laid the foundations of modern field archaeology. They dug according to their lights, and the methods they used were sometimes deplorable; but their results were outstanding, and so appealed to the popular imagination that to them we may attribute the first stirring of that general interest in archaeology on which the excavator relies today.

Egypt presented me with a problem. Practically all that we know about ancient Egyptian history—and we know a vast amount—is derived directly or indirectly from the innumerable "digs" that have been done in the Nile valley. But those digs for the most part supplement each other, every one contributing something to the picture but none of them individually illuminating history as a whole; the selection of any one might therefore seem invidious. If I have included the tomb of Tutankhamun it is because Howard Carter's discovery resulted from a sound archaeological theory directed to a particular end, and because his methods have preserved for us material beyond all parallel for the illustration of Egyptian art in a given period; and, anyhow, one could not omit Tutankhamun!

Perhaps my main difficulty was with the archaeology of the New World. There, as in Egypt, an immense amount of painstaking work has been done and a vast deal of knowledge has been accumulated regarding the Aztec, Maya, and Peruvian cultures. For a long time historians, other than the few specialists, were inclined to dicount the importance of the subject. It was held that, however remarkable in many ways were the achievements of those peoples, who at the time of the Spanish conquest were still living in the Stone Age, they themselves were dead and their works had died with them; they had exerted no formative influence upon the modern world; their arts certainly might excite our curiosity and our rather detached admiration, but from the point of view of world history possessed little interest. This was a premature conclusion. If those ancient arts were sterile it was because they had been lost in oblivion: now they have re-emerged and become familiar. Just as the rediscovery of the arts and litera-ture of classical Greece brought about the Renaissance in medieval Italy, so, possibly, may the treasures of America's past yet inspire the peoples in whose veins so much of the old blood flows to creations of which the Old World is incapable. I had no wish to undervalue the cultures of central and southern America; my problem has been to choose for description any one excavation as having been crucial for its contribution to history. Actually excavation has played but a secondary part in the discovery of the major monuments. Those of

Mexico and of Peru are often visible today, incorporated in later buildings; in the case of the Maya monuments, most of them are standing above ground but were lost in the fast-growing tropical jungle, so that their discovery (like that of the marvelous ruins of Angkor) was a matter not of excavation but of exploration. The grounds of our knowledge of them were laid by travellers such as the Englishman Maudslay, who at the end of the last century came upon so many sites and brought back squeezes of the carvings and inscriptions which he found; and today it is the air photograph, showing the ruins overtopping the trees, that leads the student to his goal. Numerous digs, conducted often on insignificant village or cemetery sites, have by combined team-work yielded valuable results, especially in establishing a comparative chronology for the wonderful pottery in which each of the great American cultures excelled, but they scarcely lent themselves to the purposes of this book. It was indeed an embarrassing choice that I had to make.

For many of my omissions I can only apologize. If my eighteen sites were to be distributed over the whole world I could scarcely afford to deal with more than one or two in any one country. Thus, for Anatolia and the history of the ancient Hittites, I hesitated between Bogazköy, the capital of their empire, Kultepe with its fascinating record of international trade, Alaca Höyük with its amazing prehistoric tombs, and Carchemish with its many sculptures and inscriptions; all had added much to our knowledge and all, except Bogazköy, where Winckler's early work had been a model of what an excavation should not be, owed a great deal of their value to modern archaeological methods. If I chose the late provincial site of Karatepe it was because there was found there the key to the Hittite inscriptions which, discovered in greater numbers on other sites, tantalized the excavator by being more or less an enigma. Of the many digs in Mesotopotamia I have chosen Ur, not because I worked there myself, but because it was the first site to yield a continuous record going back to the earliest times and to fix a relatively accurate date for periods previously unknown. For northern Syria I had planned to include M. Parrot's wonderfully successful excavation of Mari with its temples and palace in Babylonian style, its wall paintings and, above all, its political archives illustrating all the details of the administration of an ancient oriental kingdom; but Mari had to give place to Ugarit where, out of the reach of the familiar Babylonian influence, civilization developed on more independent lines.

Much as I regret the inevitable omissions, I feel sure that the digs with which the book deals will suffice to make good archaeology's proud boast that it has added new chapters to the history of man's progress the world over, and has done so by applying scientific method to mere antiquarian research. And I hope that by including two excavations carried out before scientific archaeology had been invented I have shown that method, essential though it be, is by itself not enough; the archaeologist must have imagination and sympathetic understanding if he is to make history out of his laboured record of objects and stratification and soil textures, and it was by such gifts that men like Schliemann atoned for lack of science.

Because my text is strictly limited I have tried, in the brief introduction to each subject, to sketch the necessary background and to emphasize the point, or points, in which the excavation has made a real contribution to history; for more than that there was no room. The pictures are meant to tell the story; they are the gist of the book, and I am indeed grateful to the friends who have so generously put them at my disposal. Their generosity was the greater because *History Unearthed* makes no claim to being a scientific work; but it will have been worth while if it leads some of its readers to consult the sources listed on p. 171 and to profit by their full and detailed accounts of what is here so inadequately summarized.

Nimrud

Nimrud, the mound southeast of Mosul which represents the Assyrian royal capital, Calah, has been dug twice. The site was first discovered, identified, and excavated by Layard in the 1840's, and almost exactly a century later the work was continued by the British School of Archaeology in Iraq under Professor M. E. L. Mallowan; in the interval the whole technique of scientific excavation had been developed, so that on the one spot we can see the difference between the old methods and the new.

Henry Layard was above all things an enthusiast. He had travelled widely —and at great risk—in the Middle East, wearing Oriental dress and learning the language and gradually acquiring for himself the good will and respect of the Arabs. At that time the Frenchman Botta was laying the foundations of Assyrian archaeology by his successful excavations at Kuyunjik and Khorsabad; Layard became a friend of Botta and was fired by his discoveries, which were indeed enough to inspire any man. A fortunate accident furthered his ambition. He had gone to Constantinople charged to deliver a dispatch to the British Ambassador there, Sir Stratford Canning, and because his local knowledge was of use for negotiations then in progress he remained there for two years as confidential adviser: but his archaeological enthusiasm was so contagious that when Canning was about to return to England he undertook to finance out of his own pocket a preliminary season's work at Nimrud.

In the autumn of 1846, Layard, with a few Arab workmen, began to dig what he was rightly convinced was the site of a great city; on the very first day, starting at two separate points, he discovered two of the principal palaces of the kings of Assyria. At the outset he found inscriptions only, but by the end of November was rewarded by carved stone slabs and statues. But his difficulties were great. The local authorities were obstructive, and even stopped the work for a time, and funds were running out; Canning appealed in vain to the Trustees of the British Museum and to the Treasury; it was not till Layard's own reports reached London that the importance of the work was recognized, and even then only the paltry sum of £2,000 was forthcoming. But the grant was not made unconditionally. The Museum wanted objects for exhibition; Layard found himself obliged "to obtain the largest possible number of well-preserved objects of art at the least possible outlay of time and money"; even if scientific methods had been known—and they were not—they would have had to be abandoned in view of the Trustees' demands. Layard was fully aware of the unsatisfactory nature of the work thus imposed upon him. "The smallness of the sum placed at my disposal," he wrote, "compelled me to follow the same plan in the excavations that I had hitherto adopted, viz. to dig trenches along the sides of the chambers, and to expose the whole of the slabs, without removing the earth from the centre. Thus, few of the chambers were fully explored, and many small objects of great interest may have been left undiscovered. As I was directed to bury the building with earth after I had explored it, to avoid unnecessary expense, I filled up the chambers with the rubbish taken from those subsequently uncovered, having first examined the walls, copied the inscriptions and drawn the sculptures." Fortunately Layard was a very good draftsman and his careful drawings give us a very adequate idea of the reliefs, some of which have now perished altogether; but obviously where the system was one of tunnelling, and cross measures could not be taken for checking the angle of the walls, anything like accurate planning was impossible (though Layard did his best) and no proper records could be kept, while, as the excavator complained, a great deal was left undiscovered in the centres of the rooms. Again, at that time no means had been devised for preserving such antiquities as were found; precious objects "fell to pieces … as soon as touched," or "as soon as exposed to the air," whereas today none of them would be lost; it is a sorry tale, and Layard frankly admits it. Of one loss he was unconscious. While working at Nimrud he had not yet learned what an inscribed clay tablet was, supposing them to be merely "bits of pottery decorated in an unusual manner," and whereas in his later excavations at Nineveh he discovered the royal library and brought back to London some 24,000 complete or fragmentary tablets, from Nimrud there came none at all; some at least there must have been, and one can only assume that they were discarded as rubbish.

What then was the result of Layard's dig at Nimrud, conducted as it was on methods which he himself was the first to condemn?

(1) An original drawing by Layard, done in the field

He had found, and identified, the site of the Biblical Calah and unearthed a large part of the royal palaces in it; he had discovered innumerable sculptures and had brought back to London the best preserved of them, hundreds of tons of splendid carvings which have been ever since the glory of the British Museum and for the first time introduced Assyrian art to the British public.

The colossal gate figures and the rows of wall reliefs celebrating the deeds of Assur-nasir-pal (the "Pul" of the Old Testament) did not fail to appeal to the popular imagination, and for many the culmination of it all was the Black Obelisk which pictures Shalmaneser III taking tribute from Jehu, king of Israel. Such things were not only treasures for all time, but by the interest which they aroused they made possible further work by Layard himself and by others, which was to be no less remunerative; Layard by his field work, Rawlinson by his triumphant decipherment of the inscriptions which field work brought to light, had laid the foundations of Assyriology.

In 1949, the British School of Archaeology in Iraq decided, to the surprise of many scholars, to inaugurate a fresh excavation of Nimrud. To attempt to glean where Layard had reaped so rich a harvest was indeed an act of faith: what was its justification? In the first place, Layard's palace plans were incomplete and there was still much to be learned about the layout of a royal Assyrian dwelling. Similarly, Layard unearthed parts of two palaces lying about 300 yards apart, and later the ruins of a temple of the god Nabu had been found close to one of them; but today the value of topography is better recognized and the relation between these and other buildings had to be established. Then there was the question of chronology—the accurate dating of the various buildings set up in the course of the two and a half centuries during which Calah was the imperial capital. Lastly, only three inscribed tablets were known to have been found at Nimrud (none of them by Layard) and, as Professor Mallowan wrote, "it seemed hard to believe that nothing was left of the religious library which had once been housed in the Nabu temple." For all of these problems modern methods were essential, and it is characteristic of the changed conditions that Layard's site-plan is now supplemented by air photographs.

One difference shows clearly how the aims of field archaeology have been re-oriented. Layard carried off to London the best of the monuments discovered, and buried the rest. Today not only do the reliefs stay in the country of their origin, but they are set up again in their proper setting, so that the visitor to Nimrud may see the richly-carved façade of the royal palace as it was seen in the days of the Assyrian king. The ancient city also becomes intelligible—one and a half square miles enclosed by a huge defensive wall, in the southwest of which towers the acropolis, rising forty feet above the river Tigris, its mud-brick encircling wall based, on the water side, on a quay of massive stone. Down to about 800 B.C. the temples, palaces, and houses of the more important officials were concentrated in the acropolis; later on, new royal buildings extended down into the outer town, where also there were parks and even a zoological garden! A list of the animals is given in a new and remarkable inscription that describes Assur-nasir-pal's building of his palace and the great banquet with which he celebrated the completion of his work—"sixty-nine thousand five hundred and seventy four happy peoples of all the lands for ten days I feasted, wined, bathed, and honoured them, and then sent them back to their homes in peace and joy."

The hope of finding tablets was amply fulfilled. The administrative wing of the "Northwest Palace" produced quantities of documents dealing with taxation and trade, agriculture, resettlement schemes, and reports addressed to the king on administrative questions regardin Assyria and the provinces; from the Nabu temple came hymns, incantations and omens, and medical texts, while from the throne room attached to the temple there were recovered some of the most remarkable tablets yet known, a series of treaties made by the Assyrian king Esarhaddon with princes of Iran and other neighbouring lands. Thanks to the inscriptions found in the new excavations, the chronology of the various buildings has been satisfactorily established, and in addition a mass of accurate and detailed information has enriched our knowledge of the latter days of the Assyrian empire; the tablets, as Mallowan has said, give us "a new vision of the rulers as well as the ruled: their wealth and their poverty, their wisdom and their folly."

And the contribution to art is not less striking. Layard had brought back a number of carved ivories, fragmentary and in bad condition, of which eighteen were repaired and exhibited. A far larger number were secured by Loftus, who in 1845–55 did one season's work at Nimrud, in succession to Layard. The "vast pile of unsorted fragments, calcined and often barely recognizable" were stored in the British Museum for nearly a century before the task of cleaning and fitting them together was undertaken, but even when the work was done the bulk of the collection was of more interest to the student than to the amateur of art: very few examples were more than ghosts of what they once had been. The modern excavations have produced a wealth of ivory carvings of incomparable value, often indeed fragmentary in that they had been smashed by soldiers searching for gold when in 612 B.C. the Medes sacked and burned the palaces of Calah, but preserved by careful digging and by scientific treatment so that we can appreciate both the technique and the design of these ancient masterpieces. And the best of the new Nimrud ivories, inlaid with gold and coloured stone, show us for the first time the magnificent effects aimed at by the skilled craftsmen of Sidon and of Tyre.

(2) The Rev. S. C. Malan, who visited Layard's excavations, made a number of sketches which show vividly the character of the work done. This drawing of Layard himself copying a relief illustrates just what Layard mentions in his book—"During the day, when not otherwise occupied, I made drawings of the bas-reliefs discovered in the subterranean passages." Fortunately, Layard was a skilled draftsman, so that, although many of the carved slabs were re-buried, a record of them survived.

(3) Where the debris covering the ruins was less deep, the trenches might be open to the sky. The drawing shows an entrance flanked by huge winged bulls, of which only the lower parts are exposed, beyond them a slab with a winged human figure, and in the right foreground a carved slab representing a river (flowing horizontally) with scenes on either bank. The sketch, rough and careless as it is, is yet eloquent of the unsatisfactory nature of the excavations, in this case not at Nimrud but at Nineveh.

17

(4) One of Assur-bani-pal's wall-reliefs discovered by Layard and now in the British Museum. An attack by the Assyrian forces on an enemy town on the bank of a river. The defenders man the battlements; survivors from the enemy's field force swim across the river, supported on inflated skins, trying to escape from the Assyrians, whose archers shoot at them from the wooded bank.

(5) The end of the chase. Assur-bani-pal in his chariot hunting wild bulls; one has fallen, pierced by arrows; a second, which had leaped at the chariot from behind, is killed by the king, who thrusts his weapon into its neck.

(6) The great stela of Assur-nasir-pal found
in the recent excavations at Nimrud. At the
top is the figure of the king together with
the symbols of his tutelary gods. The text
gives a summary of his conquests and then
describes in detail the building of his palace,
on which prisoners taken in battle were
employed; they were afterwards settled in
the new town as its first citizens. Then
comes a description of the canal built to
irrigate the district and of the gardens in
which were planted forty-two varieties of
fruit and gum-bearing trees brought back
from conquered countries; then an account
of the king's hunting prowess and of the live
animals kept in his zoo; and finally there is
the story of the great banquet, a story very
much like that of the feast given by King
Solomon to celebrate the building of the
Temple at Jerusalem (1 *Kings*. VIII, 65).

(7) The Black Obelisk of Shalmaneser II
is probably to be reckoned the finest individual object found by Layard at Nimrud.
In a series of twenty small reliefs, and in a
long inscription, it boasts of the tribute
brought by foreign rulers to the king of
Assyria; among those rulers was Jehu, called "the son of Omri," king of Israel, who
brought gold and silver and is portrayed
making his obeisance before his master (*see*
the second row from the top).

(8) An ivory ornament, probably for a horse's harness, carved with an Egyptian cartouche and a sphinx, which, however, is not the Egyptian sphinx (which is male), but the Syrian adaptation of the Egyptian original.

(9) The "Mona Lisa" of Nimrud, an unusually large and splendid female head carved in ivory, meant to be fastened to some piece of furniture such as the back of a throne. It was found at the bottom of a well in the palace, where it had been thrown away when the building was sacked; some of the sludge of the well still adheres to it. Many smaller heads were found, with marked characteristics representing women of different races.

(10) An ivory figure of a cow. Similar figures show that the complete carving included a calf in the space between the cow's legs; the cow turns its head to lick the little beast's hind-quarters. What is most noteworthy is the exquisitely sympathetic modelling of the mother animal.

(11) A vast deal of patient labour in the British Museum has succeeded in piecing together from the mass of ivory fragments found by Layard at Nimrud these engraved panels which originally decorated either a wooden casket or a warrior's quiver. Each of the two side strips shows a divine figure above and a beardless courtier or eunuch below; the central piece shows two such courtiers facing each other. The drawing is in the Assyrian style of the eighth century B.C.

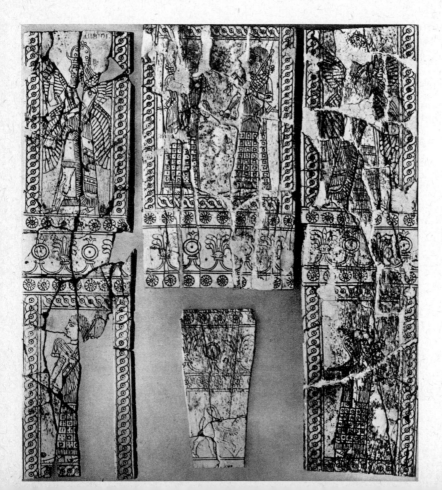

21

Troy and Mycenae

In November, 1876, Heinrich Schliemann, excavating at Mycenae, sent to the King of Greece a telegram announcing that he had discovered the body of Agamemnon. Five years before that, working on the mound of Hissarlik, which he had rightly identified with the ancient Troy, he had unearthed what he could describe as "the Treasure of Priam"; now he had before his eyes the far richer treasure placed in the tomb of the captain of the Achaean forces that had conquered Priam and sacked Troy. He had fulfilled the ambition of a lifetime.

The son of a poor German pastor, Heinrich Schliemann had as a small child been brought up on stories from Homer, and by the time he was ten years old had written a Latin essay on the events of the Trojan War. Four years later, as the grocer's assistant in the village shop, he heard a drunken man reciting Homer in the original Greek, and although he could not understand a word of it he was moved to tears by the beauty of sound and rhythm. He had promised his father that he would excavate the ruins of Troy, and always he worked to that end. Self-taught, he mastered seven foreign languages, was sent to Russia as representative of the business firm which he had joined as an office boy, and finally made a fortune. Then he learned Greek, both modern and ancient, and read and re-read his Homer in the original; he travelled, incidentally learning Arabic, and in 1859 visited Athens for the first time; then came more travelling and more successful money-making, and in his fiftieth year Schliemann began to dig at Troy.

The results of the excavations satisfied all Schliemann's dreams; he had found Homer's Troy, he had found even the treasure of Priam, king of Troy; and at once he was met with denial and derision. This could not be Troy, said some critics, because there had never been such a place outside the poet's imagination; it could not be Troy, said others, because the site of the real Troy was elsewhere; and Priam was of course a myth. Schliemann was undaunted. "I identify with the Homeric Ilion," he declared, "the city second in succession from the virgin soil" (in which he was mistaken), and he called the king Priam "because he is so called by the tradition of which Homer is the echo; but as soon as it is proved that Homer and the tradition were wrong, and that Troy's last king was called Smith, I shall at once call him so." Sceptics might dispute the identity of Troy, but of Mycenae the historical existence and the whereabouts were indisputable; so Schliemann turned his attention to Mycenae. And again he achieved a marvellous success.

Obviously the man was an enthusiast. He was a pioneer in a field of which nothing at all was known, and there were no rules to guide him, for he lived long before archaeologists had evolved anything in the way of scientific method. He made careful records of his work, but since he did not know what to look for the records were sadly incomplete; he used judgment and common-sense in insisting upon the importance of "levels," but failed to interpret them correctly. Inevitably, therefore, he made mistakes. Of the superimposed cities in the mound of Hissarlik he selected one as being Homeric Troy, and he selected the wrong one; at Mycenae he believed that he had found Agamemnon's tomb, and the tomb was centuries older than the time of Agamemnon; later scholars, working on the same sites with methods and resources then undreamed of, have demonstrated that the two claims of which he was most confident and most proud were in fact erroneous.

But those errors really detract nothing from Schliemann's credit. He had done what nobody before him had thought of doing, and just at the time when scholars, especially German scholars, had almost convinced the world that the Heroic Age of the Greeks was but a poet's dream and that its heroes were but actors in a sun-myth, he proved that the Heroic Age was a concrete fact. Objectors had dismissed the Trojan relics as mere Asiatic curiosities; but Mycenae was in Greece, and the cist graves which he discovered inside the circle of standing stones beyond the Lion Gate had been seen, and described as the graves of Agamemnon and his court, by no less a person than the Greek writer Pausanias in the second century A.D.; clearly there was, after all, a historical background to tradition. Tradition, even in Pausanias' day, had foreshortened history, but had not falsified it; the tombs are older than Agamemnon, but the Mycenaean civilization to which they belong is the pre-Homeric civilization out of which developed that of the age with which the Homeric poems deal, and if the poet harks back to the earlier period it is only because it had produced a greater art.

If we leave out the vexed question of proper names, we can wholeheartedly agree with Schliemann that he had fulfilled his ambition of bringing to light the world of the Homeric poems. From his digs there emerged a picture of an epoch in the history of Greece hitherto unsuspected. The extreme classicist might still insist that Mycenae had nothing to do with classical Hellas—that its material civilization had been that of a non-Greek people and had been utterly destroyed before ever the Greeks proper had arrived in the peninsula—but at least as a background for the great Greek epic it had surpassing interest; and it was that literary interest that had appealed to Schliemann from the beginning.

Later excavations have amply justified Schliemann's general thesis that the treasures which he found at Mycenae were of the sort that Homer described and therefore formed part of the real Greek tradition. At Mycenae itself, the late Professor Wace, carrying on Schliemann's work, unearthed in the ruins of a merchant's house inscribed clay tablets in the same "Linear B" script as those which Evans found in the later levels at Knossos, and now it has been shown that the language in which they are written is an early form of Greek; since similar tablets have been discovered elsewhere in mainland Greece, at Pylos which was the home of Nestor, one of the greatest of the Homeric heroes, the connection between the shaft tombs of Mycenae and the Iliad is indisputable. The tombs are older than the Trojan War, and Homer's epic was composed when that war was a distant memory; but the link holds good.

In Greek prehistory Schliemann was a pioneer. Nothing was known about the period which he was the first to bring to light, and he had no possible means of checking the date of what he found, so that his mistake in identifying the shaft grave as the tomb of Agamemnon was a natural one and in no way to his discredit; indeed, many years had to pass and much archaeological work to be done before it could be proved a mistake. Perhaps it was even a fortunate error, for it secured public recognition of the really great work that he had done. His was no accidental success. He had formed his plans and thought over his problems for many years; he had been guided by intuition, but also by reasonable understanding, and he worked with care as well as with enthusiasm. Granted that his technique was not that of today, he was better equipped for archaeology than have been too many of his successors, of whom it has been written that in their expedition camps "card indexes, log-books, ingenious instruments for surveying, drafting and photography were displayed with confidence and pride. Only, the fundamental canons of the craft were simply not comprehended."[1]

[1] From *Still Digging*, by Sir Mortimer Wheeler.

(12, 13) Individual objects which could be removed from the tomb and drawn at leisure by more skilled artists are much better represented; these two drawings of gold cups from the same First Grave really do give a proper idea of the things, although the carefully stippled engraving disguises all the beauty of the metal which can be rendered by a photograph.

(14) How hard put to it was an excavator at that time to secure a pictorial record of his discoveries is illustrated by this really comic effort. In the First Grave there were three bodies, of which the third wore a gold mask and gold breastplate; when these were removed the head was found to be in a remarkable state of preservation, though the body had been pressed flat and was much decayed. Schliemann hurriedly sent for a Greek painter in oils who produced this astonishing "portrait."

26

(15) Anyone who troubles to look up Schliemann's book and compares the drawing on p. 332 of the gold mask in the First Grave with the photograph published here will see how much archaeology has gained by the use of photography; in Schliemann's day the camera was indeed used, and many of the drawings were made from photographs, but there was no known means of reproducing them.

(16) From the Fourth shaft-grave came some of the finest of all the objects in the cemetery. It is curious that the gold mask covering the face of one of the five bodies is so far inferior to that from the First Grave, seeing that the objects with the body included some of the very finest from the site.

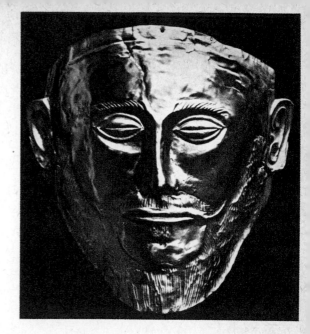

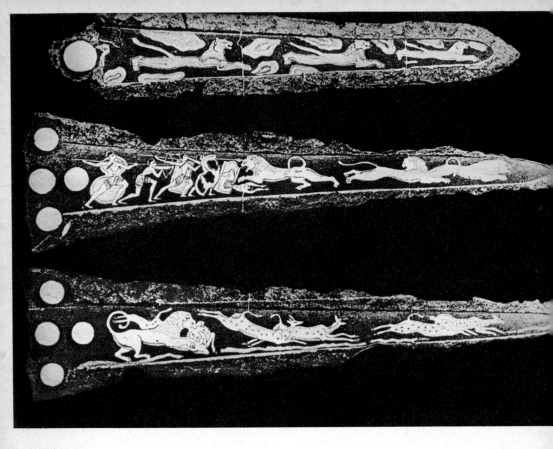

(17) The most outstanding were the bronze daggers with damascened blades. The technique of these is superb. The bronze was oxydized to a blackish-brown tint; the inlays were of gold, in two colours, a deeper red being obtained by an admixture of copper and of silver, and there was a sparing use of *niello;* the inlays were hammered in and polished and the details then engraved on them. Only in the European Renaissance were the weapons of war as exquisitely ornamented as those of Mycenae. The sub-jects, too, are admirably rendered. The cats hunting birds by the silver stream in which fishes swim might have been a fresco in the Palace of Minos in Crete; the lions chasing gazelles make a lifelike scene skilfully composed to fit the shape of the blade, and no less skilful is the scene of the lion hunt where the warriors, with their great figure-of-eight oxhide shields (compare the Knossos fresco on p. 61), are engaged in a life-and-death struggle with their wounded but still formidable prey.

28

(18) Some of the most delicate work is in the *intaglios*, engraved golden seals, of which half a dozen are shown here; and the embossed golden plaques, decorated sometimes with elaborate animal designs, sometimes with formal patterns such as spirals, are equally fine. Little amulets, animal figures in the round, adorned the dress of the warriors.

(19) A number of the bodies had diadems of gold, of which this is the most ornate. A single sheet of gold, more than two feet long and covered with embossed circular patterns, forms the diadem proper, and to its upper edge are attached quantities of small plaques, also embossed, and silhouetted to match the designs on them.

(20) A splendid object was this cow's head in silver, partly plated with gold, and with gold horns; it is about twenty inches high. It was a ritual vase, filled through a hole in the top of the head and pouring through a small hole in the muzzle. A similar vase carved in black stone comes from the palace at Knossos.

(21) A discovery that perhaps gave Schliemann more pleasure than any other was that of the gold cup figured here. It is a pedestalled chalice with two handles projecting from the rim and continued by open strapwork that runs down to the circular base, and on the top of each handle is a golden dove. It corresponds almost exactly to Homer's description of the golden cup of Nestor "which the old man had brought with him from home; a very lovely cup, studded with golden rivets; and it had four handles, on each of which were two golden doves pecking." The Mycenae chalice, urged Schliemann, has two *double* handles, which might count as four, and then the sole difference is that Nestor's cup had four doves instead of two. Here then, in the Fourth Grave, we are in direct touch with the Iliad.

Maiden Castle

We have seen how, at Nimrud and at Mycenae, excavations carried out before the days of scientific archaeology achieved success and made history by virtue of the remarkable objects which they brought to light. Maiden Castle shows us the opposite extreme. Here was a vast earthwork from which it was most unlikely that there would come a single object of artistic value; the sole purpose of the dig was to trace the character and history of mounds and ditches, and that could be done only by work on a large scale conducted with the patience and minute observation that is demanded of the modern archaeologist. The record could be obtained only by proof that one chalk embankment was older than another, that an altered line of ditch meant a changed system of defence; to secure a date series every fragment of pottery (and any stray coin, if there were any such) had to be accurately noted and, by comparison with pottery from other sites, put in its right time perspective, so that the stratum in which it occurred could be attributed to a definite period and a definite culture; if the work was not to be done with meticulous care it was not worth doing at all.

The work *was* done with meticulous care. For four years, Dr. R. E. M. Wheeler, Mrs. Tessa Wheeler and Lieut.-Col. C. D. Drew, with something like a hundred assistants and students, dug under the auspices of the Society of Antiquaries of London, spending rather more than £ 5,350; and the report published by the Society is the record of their success. It is a quite astonishing record. It must be borne in mind that virtually nothing was previously known about the site. Anybody could see at once that it was an important earthwork. In 1865, a Mr. Cunnington did some digging and found "a breast-wall of Ridgeway stones," one or two "ancient British hut-holes," several late Roman coins, a spearhead and a Roman fibula or safety pin, and fragments of pottery, etc., and he also partially excavated a "Roman villa" inside the fortifications. His casual and ill-recorded work was held to confirm the general belief that

Maiden Castle was a Roman camp: this was all that was "known," and it was all wrong. Now, thanks to the work done between 1934 and 1937, we have a complete and even dramatic chapter in the history of England; this is what the modern archaeologist could unravel from the tangle of weathered chalk mounds and filled-in ditches.

In the third millennium B.C., some of the Late Stone Age people who tilled the uplands of southern England occupied the eastern end of the saddle-backed ridge that looked down on the wooded marsh where Dorchester stands today; round their huddle of huts they dug a double ditch, more to keep their animals in than to keep enemies out, and they dug cooking pits in the surface of the chalk, and there they lived for a long time. But gradually the population diminished; the ditches had been virtually filled in flat with the ashes of the fires men burned in them and by the weathering of the chalk sides, and at last the settlement was abandoned. But it was not forgotten. From the centre of the twelve-acre enclosure along the highest contour of the ridge there is a long mound made up of the chalk and soil thrown up from the two trenches that flank it on either side; it had been something more than five feet high, about sixty feet wide, and no less than 1,790 feet long; toward its eastern end was a grave containing the body of a man whose legs, arms, and head had been cut off after his death and the skull opened to remove the brain. In the longest "Long Barrow" known in England there was evidence of some grim ritual, probably cannibalistic, practised by our Neolithic ancestors. And soon after this remarkable burial (perhaps attracted by it?) the Stone Age people came back, set up their huts, and used the shelter of the ditches of the Long Barrow for their kitchen fires; but they were a peaceable folk, or in that thinly populated land had no reason to fear attack, so that they did nothing to make good the bank and ditches that surrounded the old village. While they lived there, the world was changing and the Late Stone Age was giving place to the Bronze Age. In the filling of the Long Barrow ditches the Neolithic potsherds become mixed with and then outnumbered by fragments of the beakers and grooved or collared food vessels of the fully developed Bronze Age culture, and that so abruptly that we must suppose not that the old-fashioned villagers began to import the better wares manufactured by neighbours, but that an influx of Bronze Age "beaker" people joined with or replaced the Neolithic stock. But they did not remain very long. The Long Barrow would seem to have been built not earlier than 2000 B.C., and the "beaker people" arrived two or three centuries later; but by about 1500 B.C., they had gone. There is evidence to show that at about that time the climate of this island changed and became drier. What had been swamps or peat bogs became fit for human occupation, and in the lowlands the area of cultivatable land was increased; man therefore moved down from the hill-tops. The Bronze Age shepherd may still have driven his flocks to pasture on the sweet grass of the chalk downs, but the villages now lay in the plains; for about twelve hundred years Maiden Castle was deserted.

By about 300 B.C., things changed again. The agricultural population had increased greatly in numbers and was swelled by immigrants from the continent who at first settled down peacefully on unoccupied land, but in time there were too many to be supported by the scattered strips of arable soil in the wooded valleys; and at this time, too, the weather changed again and a moister climate made easy the resettlement of the wide spaces of the downs.

The Bronze Age had passed, and Europe was now in the Early Iron Age. From Normandy groups of immigrants, "displaced persons," Iron Age people who derived their culture ultimately from Hallstatt in Austria, landed on the Wessex coast and in time occupied Maiden Castle. But as people accustomed to trouble, they proceeded to fortify their settlement upon European lines; the site they chose was that of the Neolithic village, but they extended its area to about sixteen acres and enclosed it with a wall ten or twelve feet high of earth and chalk, retained back and front by timbering held in place by ten-inch posts five feet apart; in front of the wall was a berm or level strip and then a ditch fifty feet wide and twenty feet deep. At either end there was a gateway, a double one with two gates at the east end and a single one at the west; outside the east gate there was a metalled area with pens for cattle, perhaps a market place. The houses inside the ramparts were pit dwellings cut into the chalk and roofed over.

Actually no enemies attacked this early stronghold and the walls were allowed to fall into disrepair, which may well have happened within fifty years. But the population grew in numbers and the old limits were too narrow, so towards 200 B.C. the "town" was enlarged to the west so as to include an area of forty-six acres; and this addition, as well as the old part, was surrounded by a wall and ditch. For this, a new principle was adopted. There was no wall with vertical timber facing (which had been proved a failure) and no berm; the new rampart was merely a heap of chalk rubble and earth whose outer slope continued the slope of the ditch, forming thus a *glacis* which would stop any rush attack and leave an exhausted assailant at the mercy of the defenders; and now, if not earlier, the gates were strengthened by a barbican, a triangle of mound and ditch jutting out from the main line with two passageways through it and flanking enclosures which gave opportunity for a crossfire on invaders.

Toward the middle of the first century B.C., a new body of intruders came to Maiden Castle and, although apparently not very numerous, assumed control of the former inhabitants. The first thing they did was to remodel the defences. They rebuilt the main rampart on twice its original scale, its slopes of chalk and earth strengthened by internal walls, the upper part of its inner face revetted first with chalk and later with limestone; the outer face ran down into the ditch at a slope of forty degrees and formed a slippery ramp eighty feet long. On the steep slope along the north side of the fort one, and on the flatter area to the south, two new lines of mound and ditch were added beyond the lip of the greatly enlarged old moat, and the two gateways were elaborated with a complicated system of earthworks to guard their entrances; the total width of the defence lines was now about 100 yards on the north and on the more vulnerable south side 140 yards. The reason for this is clear. The newcomers were above all sling-men, and the range of a sling-stone was anything up to 200 yards; an enemy therefore was within range from the moment that he attempted to rush the defences, and until he had got well within them his own shots could not reach the interior of the town; new weapons called for new defence tactics.

It is probable that the newcomers were men of the tribe of the Veneti from Brittany who had long been, as tin traders, in touch with Cornwall and now, seeking a new home perhaps because of Caesar's punishment of the tribe for their resistance to Rome in 56 B.C., chose the more fertile downs of Dorset. The Veneti were skilled sling-men who in Brittany had learned the value of multiple lines of defence, so that the changes they made at Maiden Castle are easily explained.

There was to be a further change. About twenty years after the beginning of our era the Belgae who were settled in Kent and Sussex but had been gradually expanding westward—possibly because they were hard pressed by the territorial ambitions of Cunobelinus of Colchester (Shakespeare's Cymbeline)—reached the Test Valley and then made a further push which brought them into Wessex. Between 25 and 30 A. D., they secured Maiden Castle, as is proved by both pottery and Belgic coins. At once the defences were brought up to date. The outer ditches and ramparts added by the Veneti were remodelled on the same gigantic scale as the main line; the gateway approaches were redesigned with roads that zigzagged between and were commanded by interlocking outworks, which included masonry platforms and towers, and in the walls, too, there was a free use of heavy stones; along the top of the inner rampart ran a palisade of stout posts and hurdles. Military discipline affected the entire town. The whole area within the walls had been honeycombed with pits of all sorts—dwelling-pits, store-pits, cooking-pits, and refuse-pits alongside or underneath the surface huts; all were now filled in, a clean sweep made of what must have been a foul mess, and new huts were set up all over the site. But the end came very soon. In the year A. D. 47, Vespasian, the future emperor of Rome, advanced with the legions into Dorset. At Maiden Castle the Roman infantry, covered by a barrage of iron-shod ballista-arrows, fought their way up to the eastern gate. Some huts had been built here outside the actual gateway; the Romans set them on fire and, masked by the smoke, stormed the gates, burst into the town, and started a massacre of the inhabitants. Then they dismantled the gates, tore down the palisades, and withdrew to their camp, leaving the survivors to bury under cover of night the bodies of those who had fallen; nineteen centuries later, the excavators were to find those graves, hastily dug in the hot ashes of the huts outside the ruined gateways. For twenty years or so, a few still lived on in the now defenceless town, but then, as Roman Dorchester arose on the plain below, it was formally and finally abandoned. Three hundred years later, just before the end of the Roman period, someone built on Maiden Castle a little Romano-Celtic temple with a humble priest's house alongside, close to what may have been on older hut; but that was all, and it only accentuated the desolation of the site. This was the "villa" on the strength of which Mr. Cunnington identified Maiden Castle as a Roman camp.

In their reconstruction of history the excavators, of course, were utilizing the results of many other digs both in England and on the Continent for the classification and dating of pottery and for parallels afforded by the Bronze Age earthworks, etc. But this would have been useless if the actual work at Maiden Castle had not been conducted on the most scientific lines. Only when the almost inextricable tangle of mounds and ditches had been unravelled could the character of the defences at any one period be established, and only when the stratum of every potsherd and its relation to the building-phase had been put on record could it be cited as evidence for date or culture. As it is, the completeness of the history is a striking testimony to the value of archaeological methods.

(22) The air photograph of Maiden Castle from the west shows us the general layout of the multiple earthworks which cover and enclose the saddle-backed hill that rises two miles south-west of Dorchester, perhaps the most imposing of all the earthworks of England. The mounds and ditches are those of the latest period, just before the Roman invasion, most of the earlier defences being buried beneath or cut away by the massive lines of the Belgic fortress. It will be noticed that on the north side where the slope of the hill is steeper, two great ditches were deemed sufficient, while on the gentler southern slope a third is added for better protection.

The series of white strips across the hill-top are the trenches cut by the excavators to follow the course of the enormous "long barrow" of Neolithic times.

(23) A photograph looking along the inner ditch on the north side of the fortress shows its huge scale. The ramparts have been weathered down and the debris from them has filled the ditch to a depth of over seven feet; but even in their present state they bear witness to the immense amount of labour that went to the making of these defences.

(24) The horn-work of the eastern entrance in the first phase of the Iron Age occupation. The wall of chalk slabs and earth originally ten or twelve feet high and strengthened with strong posts and timbering (the timbering has gone but the gaps left by the posts are clear enough) served as a revetment for the inner mound; in front of it is the level "berm," and at the bottom of the photograph can be seen the lip of the great ditch.

(25) A section cut in the inner slope of the main rampart of the later phase of the Iron Age occupation. The height of the mound was now increased by about eight feet, and the new work was secured by an elaborate system of internal walls of chalk blocks. The actual surface slope of the mound can be seen on the right of the photograph; on the left are post-holes and rough rubble walling which kept the filling in place while it was being flung up above the old rampart; behind it is the next internal wall built in the core of the mound, and at the top a man points to the holes left by the wooden palisade which, in the last phase, the Belgae set up along the crown of the rampart.

(26) It has been said that the great increase in the depth of the defences was dictated by the character of the weapons used by the garrison of the fortress. The newcomers to Wessex were armed primarily with slings, and so required a good field of fire and a suitable range. They needed also good stocks of missiles, and at various points of the defence line there were found hoards of sling-stones; here is one such magazine, close to the eastern entrance, which contained over 20,000 stones.

(27) Between the horn-work and the southern portal of the eastern entrance is the war cemetery where, on the night after the Roman capture of the fort, the Belgic survivors buried those who had fallen in the gate's defence. The view is taken from the south; the level in the middle is roughly that of the Belgic roadway, into which the graves were cut; on the right a workman stands on the roadway of the earlier Iron Age, and beyond him can be seen the post-and-rubble revetment of the rampart end flanking the entry proper.

(28) A grave in the war cemetery. The skeleton is that of a woman, suggesting either that women took part in the defence or that victory was followed by a massacre of the inhabitants. The arms are bent behind the body, possibly bound at the time of her death, and she seems to have been killed by three blows on the head which cut away part of the bone. In her left hand she holds a leg of lamb; in this, as in many other cases, a pathetic attempt had been made, in all the hurry and secrecy of the midnight burials, to give to the dead some offering of respect, some provision for their long journey.

(29) The survivors who still occupied the dismantled fortress laid down a new road through the south portal of the eastern entrance. In the photograph, the lower-level surface marked A is that of the Belgic roadway, and on the right of it are the scanty remains of the flanking wall; B marks the road-surface of the early Roman time, and, as can be seen, it rests upon a litter of loose stone blocks; they are the blocks torn down from the flanking walls when the Roman soldiers dismantled the place, and they still lie where they fell then.

In the background is a rough stone wall built here late in the Roman period to block the south portal; it is probably contemporary with the little Roman temple.

(30) Soon after the middle of the fourth century A.D., on the long-deserted hill-top there was built a small temple of normal Romano-Celtic type, with a square sanctuary measuring sixteen feet either way surrounded by a veranda with low walls carrying, probably, wooden dwarf columns. Close to it was a little two-roomed building, a house for the temple's priest, while an oval hut on the other side of the temple may possibly have replaced an older shrine. The photograph shows the temple, with the priest's house beyond it, on ground honeycombed with the old Iron Age pits. It was the last building to be put up within the walls of Maiden Castle, and it did not last long. It was roughly repaired in the reign of Theodosius 383–95 (A.D.), but the latest coin out of about a hundred found in it was of Honorius (393–423 A.D.), and we may conclude that with the collapse of the Roman regime the temple was abandoned and Maiden Castle relapsed into solitude.

(31) Of two men buried together in one grave, one had three cuts in the head and, in addition, his skull was pierced by a square-headed arrow, probably a bolt from a Roman *ballista*, or catapult. The second man had an iron arrowhead fixed in his vertebra; the point had entered the body from in front, below the heart, and he had then been finished off with a sword cut across the head.

The Fayum and Oxyrhynchus

It was in 1778 that the first Greek manuscript written on Egyptian papyrus reached Europe. Peasants had found it in the Fayum, the great depression west of the Nile valley which had in antiquity been covered by the waters of Lake Moeris, but had been drained and brought under control in Ptolemaic times and had become an immensely rich agricultural province, dotted with towns and villages and rural temples; it is still rich and populous, and can be described as "a green carpet on the tawny Libyan desert." The Greek manuscript came from the ruins of one of the towns; it was one of about fifty rolls found all together, but the rest of them were burned by the peasants "because they liked the aromatic smell!" and for a hundred years all such treasures as they chanced to find went the same way.

But in 1877, a large dump—perhaps the waste paper thrown out from some official record-office of the Graeco-Roman period—was discovered in the ruins of Arsinoë, the provincial capital, and these began to find a market in Vienna and Berlin, London and Paris; so the natives set to work and for twenty years plundered the Fayum sites. Some of the diggers, more interested in statues and statuettes, which sold more readily, did not bother to keep such things as manuscripts, and even when they did, because papyri are extremely fragile and the diggers' methods were of the roughest sort, not nearly half of what they unearthed was preserved. But in the years 1888-90, Flinders Petrie, the founder of modern archaeology in Egypt, was excavating at Hawâra, close to the Ptolemaic dam that controlled the lake waters (see the maps on p. 43) and came upon papyri. His discovery started a new era. In 1895-96, the Egypt Exploration Fund sent out an expedition to the Fayum expressly to dig for papyri; and thereafter, for year after year, Grenfell and Hunt—they became an almost legendary pair—carried on work first in the Fayum and afterwards at Behnesa, the ancient Oxyrhynchus, on the western edge of the desert, 120 miles south of Cairo.

The bulk of the papyri are found either in the ruins of houses or in the town rubbish heaps. Sometimes, especially in the houses of priests, there might be magazines in which manuscripts were stored; more often the papers were simply left behind by the owners when the house was given up; then the walls fell in, and any rubbish left upon the floors was thus sealed up and preserved.

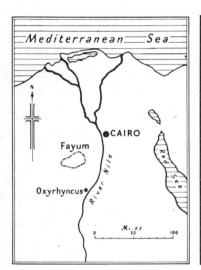

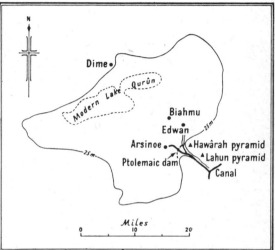

Naturally, people did not always leave things behind; but when, as happened in the case of a village named Dimê, the site lay far out in the blue, dependent on a single canal for its domestic water and for the irrigation of its land, and that canal suddenly failed, then the inhabitants went off in a hurry and the modern excavator is rewarded by a rich harvest of papyri.

To dig a town rubbish-heap in the hope of finding "waste paper" might seem to show excessive optimism, and it is true that the search may be un-remunerative; but Grenfell and Hunt soon learned that in fact not much work is needed to tell the excavator whether the dig is going to be worth while or not. For some reason or another papyri are only found—or are only found in good condition—in layers of a peculiar sort of rubbish which the digger after a very little experience can easily recognize; if there is no such layer in the rubbish-mound he stops work; if the layer is there, he digs on hopefully, and more often than not "strikes oil."

But there are other sources of papyri.

Flinders Petrie discovered at Gurob, and later Grenfell and Hunt discovered at Umm et Baragât, cemeteries of the Ptolemaic period in which the dead had been embalmed in old Egyptian fashion and placed in mummy-cases, modelled and painted. Examining these, Petrie discovered that the head-pieces and breast-covers of the cases were made of a sort of cartonnage; the oldest consisted of pieces of linen cloth which had been glued and pressed together on a mould, then covered with stucco and painted; later on, papyrus was glued and coated and painted in the same way; but still later, the sheets of papyrus were only soaked and pressed together—and with care those sheets could be separated and, especially where the papyrus was flat, as on the breast-pieces, might produce precious texts. And such texts were not necessarily just odd scraps. "The Egyptian undertaker," wrote Grenfell, "before making a mummy-case, bought the waste-paper basket of one of his neighbours and turned the papers that were in it into papier-mâché for the particular mummy-case he had in hand; thus the papyri coming from a particular mummy all belong to one collection."

To recover ancient manuscripts by pulling coffins to pieces is surely one of the curiosities of archaeology; but something yet more curious was to follow. Throughout the ancient Fayum, the crocodile had been an object of worship, and Grenfell and Hunt found a cemetery in which the sacred beasts, properly embalmed, had been ceremoniously buried. The embalmers had removed the animals' entrails, and then, to preserve their shape, had stuffed them with papyrus rolls! Samson is said to have got honey out of the body of a dead lion, but it was left for the modern scholar to extract Greek poetry from the stomach of a crocodile.

But what was it that mummies, crocodiles, and rubbish-mounds contributed to our knowledge?

When the results of the first season in the Fayum were reported, Professor Sayce was reminded of the days when the fall of Constantinople brought Greek literature to Italy and started the Renaissance. "The fortunate excavator," he wrote, "has disinterred classical Greek papyri of an age of which the most sanguine scholar had not ventured to dream; he has found private correspondence which throws light on the social history of the Greek settlers in Egypt in the early days of the Ptolemaic dynasty, records of wills which will cast a most important light on Greek law, private accounts which inform us of the prices and taxation in the Fayum in the third century B.C., a portion of a lost play by Euripides and last, but not least, fragments of a precious copy of the *Phaedo* of Plato, which must have been written not long after the time of the philosopher himself.''

The Fayum towns were small and their inhabitants, agriculturalists for the most part, would not have been greatly interested in literature. Grenfell and Hunt moved on to Oxyrhynchus, which had been an important city, the home of rich people who might well have had libraries of their own. Few sites could have seemed more hopeless to the ordinary archaeologist. For centuries the inhabitants of Behnesa, the modern town, had plundered the ruins for stones and bricks wherewith to build their own houses; of the old buildings not a wall, scarcely a wall-foundation survived; only the rubbish-heaps were undisturbed. There Grenfell and Hunt dug, looking always for the curiously-coloured layer which experience had taught them should be fruitful, and their success was astonishing. One day, thirty-six baskets were brought into the expedition house, all full of papyrus rolls some of which measured from three to ten feet in length; and there were twenty-five basketfuls on the following day. Once there was found, running through the rubbish, a thick layer consisting entirely of papyrus rolls—there were even the old baskets which had been flung out on to the heap with the papyri still in them—unluckily torn up first, so that the baskets might hold more. It was an amazing harvest.

None of the Oxyrhynchus papyri was Ptolemaic; the earliest dated from the Roman conquest of Egypt and the latest came down to the eighth or ninth century A.D. Naturally the "waste paper" was of all sorts, and the dozens of volumes since published show us documents of every kind, from the letter of a schoolboy demanding more pocket-money and a cake to a contract (dated 550 A.D.) whereby a horse-trainer takes over the management of Flavius Serenus' racing-stables, reports sent by and orders given to estate agents, wills, police orders, "appeals unto Caesar"—these were the kind of thing that one might perhaps have expected. But as the excavators had hoped, some of the citizens of the Roman town had been of a literary turn of mind. Page after page of Homer came to light, approving or emending our received text; new poems by Sappho and by Alcaeus, the early Greek lyric writers; fragments of the great dramatic writers and of the orators; for the classical scholar it was a gold-mine. But some of the citizens had been Christians, and that at an early date; a copy of the first chapter of St. Matthew's Gospel was probably written in the third century A.D.; part of St. Mark's Gospel was later (fifth-sixth century), yet even so it is one of our earliest texts. But of far more general appeal was that which at once became famous as the *Logia*, the *Sayings of Jesus*. The principal fragment, shown on Plate I, was a page from a collection of the sayings of Our Lord, the sort of collection that the writers of the Gospels may well have used when setting in order the story of Christ's ministry; the document, according to the excavators, is somewhat earlier than the year 240 A.D. and therefore should embody a very direct memory. Most of the Sayings preserved are familiar to us, repeating what we have in the canonical books; but one is altogether new. "Jesus saith; Wherever there are two, they are not without God, and wherever there is one alone, I say, I am with him. Raise the stone and there thou shalt find me, cleave the wood and there am I."

(32) This is the famous papyrus found in the first season at Oxyrhynchus. It is a single page from a book; one or two lines at the bottom are missing, and on one side much of the writing is terribly rubbed and in part obliterated. The Saying quoted above comes on the right-hand side, beginning at the second line. The following Saying runs, "Jesus saith, A prophet is not acceptable in his own country, neither doth a physician work cures upon them that know him."

PLATE I

(33) In the next season, Grenfell and Hunt discovered this fragment of another collection of "The Sayings of Jesus." It consisted of forty-two incomplete lines written on the back of a survey list of lands drawn up in the late second or early third century A.D.; it had been a roll, probably a long roll. The Sayings were written about 250 A.D. The text begins with an introduction, "These are the ... words which Jesus the living lord spake to ... and to Thomas, and he said unto them 'Every one that hearkens to these words shall never taste of death.'" Since not much more than half of each line is preserved, the true reading is often doubtful; but the first Saying can be restored with tolerable certainty —"Jesus saith, Let not him who seeks ... cease until he finds, and when he finds he shall be astonished; astonished he shall reach the kingdom, and having reached the kingdom he shall rest."

Anyang

Medicine in China a hundred years ago was very much like that of fifteenth-century Europe, a very little science combined with a great deal of magic. The chemist might compound his own drugs, or he might sell the ingredients to be made up by the doctor or the patient; the mixture might be arbitrary, but the several ingredients were those approved either by experience or by superstition. One of the most potent drugs in the pharmacopœia was "dragons' bones," and these were naturally rare and expensive.

It was about 1860 that the farmers of Hsiao T'un, in the Chinese province of Honan, began to find in their fields fragments of peculiar bones which had a very fine polished surface, were marked with oval notches and T-shaped cracks and sometimes were engraved with rows of queer geometrical-looking signs or even tiny pictures. One of the farmers, Li by name, decided that these could be nothing other than dragons' bones, so he collected all he could and offered them for sale to a chemist, who gladly bought such unquestionable relics; for thirty years Li carried on a very lucrative trade, and the chemists also profited, for the powdered bones were believed to be invaluable for nervous complaints.

But in 1899, a Chinese antiquary noticed in a shop some of the unpowdered bones and realized that the curious marks upon them were writing—Chinese writing, but of a sort so archaic that neither he nor anybody else could read them. Where they came from nobody could say, for Li kept his trade secret, but since they were obviously of scientific interest the inscribed bones were eagerly bought up by scholars; but it was only after thirty years of study that the inscriptions upon them could be fully explained.

The bones were ancient "oracle bones." You had the question to which you required an answer engraved upon a bone or a tortoise shell by a priest who then made notches in certain places and applied heat so that the bone (or shell) cracked, and from the direction taken by the crack he could deduce the reply, "yes" or "no"; sometimes the priest wrote the answer on the bone, and he might even add a note saying that the answer had been proved correct. The thousands of bones which by now had been salved from the chemical laboratory all belonged to the royal archives—the questions were the king's questions, dealing with politics or war or, more often, with the crops, inquiring what weather was to be expected and what were the prospects of harvest; and the kings who thus consulted the oracles were those of the Shang Dynasty, which ruled this part of China between 1765 and 1123 B.C. How important that was for the history of China can easily be shown. When, in 1911, the professor of Chinese in the University of Cambridge published a book on *The Civilisation of China from the Earliest Times* he began at 1000 B.C.; but even so, his account of "The Feudal Ages", which goes down to 220 B.C., takes only a few pages. The same professor, reviewing a book on *The Ancient History of China* by another authority describes it as "a sketch of the fabulous ages down to 221 B.C., containing a good deal of information of an antiquarian character, and altogether placing in its most attractive light what must necessarily be rather a dull period for the general reader." Twenty-five years later, in 1936, Dr. Creel, writing on *The Birth of China*, devotes more than two hundred pages to the Shang period, 1765–1123 B.C., and his description is of absorbing interest. This revolution in knowledge and in outlook is largely due to the oracle bones.

When the peasants of Hsiao T'un discovered that the bones in their fields were more valuable as antiques than as medicines they began to dig for them instead of merely collecting what lay on the surface, and in digging they found more than they had expected. As might have been guessed from the fact that the oracles belonged to the royal archives, the site on which they were found was that of the royal capital of the Shang kings, a city called Anyang or (later) Lin. The plunderers of course paid no attention to any remains of buildings, but digging more deeply they came upon tombs containing treasures of all sorts and, in particular, magnificent bronze vessels enriched with elaborate decoration in relief and sometimes bearing inscriptions of a historical character. Because these things came from clandestine diggings and nothing could be learned about the conditions in which they were found (indeed, it was a long time before scholars could discover that the fine objects to be bought in the shops of the Peking dealers came from Anyang), much of the historical value of these treasures was lost and even the date to which they should be assigned was a matter of dispute. But at last the truth leaked out, and in 1928 regular excavations on the Anyang site were started by the Freer Gallery of Art, U. S. A., and the National Research Institute of China. From the outset, fierce opposition by the peasants (or "bandits"), who saw that the source of their wealth was threatened, hampered the excavators, and then the Japanese invasion of 1936, and civil war, made digging impossible; but a great deal had been done, and when conditions allowed the work was resumed by the Chinese Government, and still continues.

(34) Until the arrival of the Shang people, this part of China was still in the Stone Age. Excavation has brought to light the houses of these barbarians, circular dugouts with roofs of reed or matting supported by posts. Here can be seen a dug-out of the sort, with its post-holes and central hearth. The curious pot-like things in the background are other post-holes which have been carefully preserved by digging round them when the excavation was carried down to deeper levels.

(35) A view looking down into a royal tomb. Two stepped approaches lead down to the bottom of a square shaft cut in the soil, and in the middle of that is the pit for the royal burial. Round the pit, and in the approach passages, lie the offerings made to the dead and the bodies of the members of his household who accompanied the king to the other world.

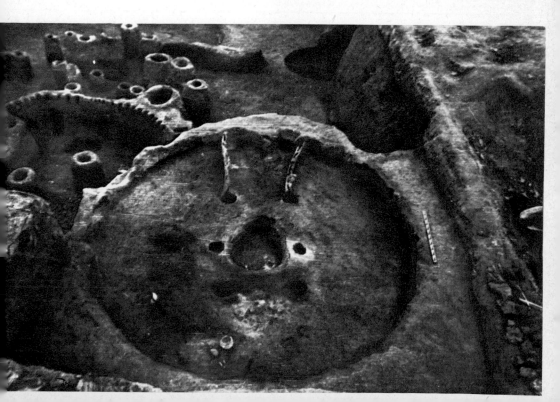

(37) The white object that can be seen on plate 35 close to the left-hand side of the inner pit is this large and beautifully carved piece of jade. It is difficult to say what purpose it served, but jade was a material always prized by the Chinese, and a fine piece so exquisitely carved was in itself something of which any king might be proud.

(36) Here are examples of the oracle bones of Anyang. The notches or holes show where the heat was applied to produce the cracks which gave the answer to the question.

(38) In some of the later graves the great man was buried in his horse-drawn chariot. Here can be seen the skeletons of the horses and the driver, and although the woodwork of the chariot has decayed away entirely, yet the impression of it left in the earth is very clear. It was a two-wheeled vehicle with a heavy pole which projected behind the wheels to support the body of the car.

(39) The traces were strung with large beads (a fashion which prevailed at Ur also) and over the necks of the horses rose a tall object, a bronze fork with a knob at the top which was probably for ornament only.

53

(40) But the finest objects in the Anyang tombs were the bronze vessels, of which two examples are shown here. Richly decorated with over-all patterns in low relief and sometimes with boldly outstanding figures, these are masterpieces of the technique of bronze-casting by the *cire perdue* process, while as works of art they are not surpassed by Chinese work of any later date.

(41) This splendid bronze ritual vessel was not found in any properly conducted excavation but, as is only too often the case, was looted by tomb robbers, so that all record of its associations is lost; but on grounds of style it can safely be attributed to Anyang. Because its surface is so well preserved it shows most clearly the bold and yet delicate workmanship of the old Chinese bronze caster and the beauty of his design.

(42) It may well be that the Chinese learned the technique of bronze-casting from others, but none the less did they use it for an art peculiarly their own. Thus the curious legs of the bronze vessels are at once explained if we look at such a clay vase as this; three pots with pointed bases were joined together at an angle to make a sort of tripod. It is a type which in China goes right back to the Stone Age. When the craftsman learned how to use metal he employed the new material for shapes that were traditionally and essentially Chinese.

Knossos

In the early eighties of last century, Schliemann, fresh from his triumphs at Troy and Mycenae, turned his attention to Crete, attracted there partly by Greek legends (which however have nothing to say about the great Minoan civilization) and partly by geographical considerations; but political difficulties made it impossible for him to dig. In 1893, Arthur Evans announced to the Hellenic Society a startling discovery; numerous engraved seal-stones, supposed to have originated in the Greek Peloponnese, had been traced by him to Crete, and on them he had distinguished pictographic signs which convinced him that in prehistoric Crete the art of writing was known. Evans felt all the force of the arguments that had appealed to Schliemann—he, too, wanted to find out what lay behind the traditions of Minos and Daedalus and the fabled Labyrinth, but in addition his quest of an early form of writing led him to the island. He decided that a hillock inland from Candia, where surface finds had been made even in Schliemann's time, offered most promise; by an act of faith he purchased the site of Knossos, and in 1900, when conditions were more peaceful, he began to excavate it.

In the very first season astonishing treasures came to light, and among them quantities of clay tablets—tablets of unbaked clay, but fortunately hardened by the fire which had destroyed the building—inscribed with the unknown script which he had foreseen. In later seasons more tablets were found at Knossos—more than 1,600 in all—and others turned up at Phaestus, on the south side of the island, and at Mallia; others were unearthed on the Greek mainland, at Orchomenos, Pylos and Mycenae, and it was evident that the Minoan Cretans had invented a system of writing the use of which in time spread over the whole of the Mycenaean world.

Evans distinguished three forms of the script. The earliest was purely hieroglyphic, and out of this there were evolved two cursive types. One of them, "Linear A," was used at Knossos in its great days and down to about 1400 B.C., when Crete was over-run by the Mycenaeans; the other, "Linear B," was taken over by the Mycenaeans and used by them on the Greek mainland as well as in Crete up to the time of their collapse about 1200 B.C. Evans had therefore achieved his ambition. He had traced the Mycenaean civilization which Schliemann had discovered back to its source in Crete, and he had proved that both civilizations practised the art of writing.

The Minoan civilization, as illustrated by Evans' discoveries, took the world by surprise. Some elements of it could be attributed to Egypt, on the one side, to Asia on the other; but all such borrowings had been assimilated by the genius of the Cretan people and transmuted into an original and individual art. Architecturally, a Cretan palace was unlike the buildings of any other land; it was magnificent in design and technique, peculiarly adapted to the island climate and to the islanders' way of living, and in some respects, such as drainage and water supply, was superior to anything that Europe could produce until the nineteenth century A.D.; its decoration was superb, the walls adorned with frescoes which were masterpieces of painting, while their spirit bore witness to a *joie de vivre* totally at variance with the pompous arrogance of later Mesopotamia and with the preoccupation with another world and the nostalgia of contemporary Egypt. Minoan art, whether shown in the delicate carvings in ivory, in the bronzes, or in the humbler field of painted pottery, is always individual to Crete and displays a love of beauty for its own sake, a real aesthetic sense, which we only too often fail to find in the other civilizations of the ancient world.

Knossos was a revelation. But the question arose, did it greatly matter? Was this but an isolated triumph of human genius, confined to one small island and to one relatively short space of time, or did it in truth contribute to the history of man's progress? Evans stoutly maintained that it did, that here we had a forerunner of Greece whose achievements helped to explain the marvels of the classical age; Athenian art of the fifth century B. C. traced its descent ultimately to Cretan art of the second millennium. Many archaeologists agreed with Evans from the outset, but the claim he made was a stumbling block for scholars of the older school; for them, just as Athena was said to have sprung fully armed from the head of Zeus, so the civilization of classical Greece had no antecedents but was the spontaneous outcome of sixth-century Attic genius. I remember Evans trying to convert one famous classical authority, displaying before him the treasures from Knossos then in the Ashmolean Museum; the scholar listened and at last, with a smile half-indulgent and half-contemptuous, answered with a Shakespearean pun, "Yes, Evans, a poor thing, but Minoan!" For him, Knossos was something alien and apart and therefore of little interest: granted that Crete created Mycenae, still that meant nothing; Mycenae had been swept out of existence by the Achaeans and, apart from legends, had left no trace of itself in later history; between Mycenae and classical Greece, and *a fortiori* between Crete and classical Greece, there was nothing in common.

Then, in 1953, the unexpected happened. Michael Ventris, a young architect with keen archaeological interests, announced that, in collaboration with John Chadwick, he had unravelled the secret of the Cretan Linear B script; the mysterious tablets could be read, and the language in which they were written was Greek!

Scholars the world over, with no exception worth mentioning, have accepted Ventris' conclusions, and the results are far-reaching. We do not yet know whether or not the language of the purely Cretan Linear A script also is Greek, but however that may be, Evans' thesis is vindicated. Long before 1400 B. C., the Mycenaeans of Greece, probably as subjects of Minos, had assimilated Cretan art so thoroughly that the modern archaeologist is sometimes at a loss to decide whether an object unearthed at Mycenae, Tiryns, or Pylos was manufactured locally or was an import from Knossos. In the minor arts, such as pottery, the workmanship was necessarily provincial, and what started as copies developed into a distinct school which we call Mycenaean, as opposed to

Cretan; but this is merely an offshoot of the parent stock. When the Mycenaeans in 1400 B.C. overthrew the Minoan overlordship they transferred the political power to their mainland centres; but there they maintained a culture which was fundamentally Cretan. And they themselves were Greeks. With that crucial discovery, the link between Knossos and Athens is established.

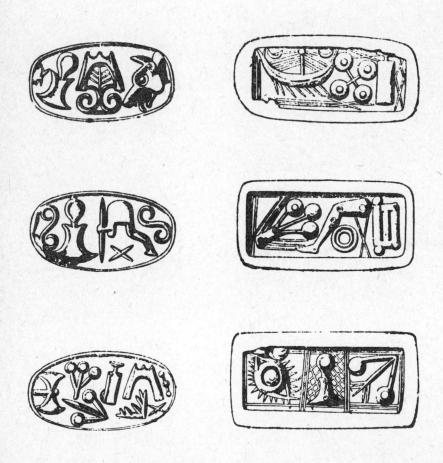

(44, 45) In 1900, after six years of excavation, Evans' search proved successful; complete hoards of inscribed clay tablets were found. The bulk of them, written in what is called the Linear B script, the third type of writing to be employed at Knossos, were inventories of palace property—records of stores of grain, tools, chariots or parts of chariots, or lists of men and women presumably engaged in the royal service. The larger of the two tablets shown here is of a different type, and Evans suggested that it might be a contract or legal formula.

◄

(43) Here are examples of Cretan seals engraved with patterns in which Evans recognized pictographs or hieroglyphic signs implying a system of writing; this was what led him to dig in Crete.

(47) The original appearance of the interior of the palace is shown by this restored drawing of the West Porch; walls and ceiling alike are covered with gay paintings, among which is a bull-fighting scene (left).

(46) The dignity and splendor of Minoan architecture is illustrated by this restored drawing of a *loggia* opposite the Grand Staircase of the palace. The tapered wooden column-shafts are thicker at the top than at the base—their shape was proved by taking plaster casts of the holes left in the hard soil by the decay of the wood. Halfway up the wall was a painted band of spiral decoration against which are seen the big figure-of-eight shields carried by Cretan soldiers; here the dappled ox-hide shields are only painted, but in some cases actual shields were hung up against a similar band of ornament. The whole place was a blaze of colour.

60

(48) The piecing together of fragments of fallen frescoes was a difficult business; inevitably, much had disappeared altogether, reduced to powder; but although some restoration was always needed, entire scenes were recovered and gave a vivid idea of the palace decoration. Here is a girl toreador, in the act of alighting after her leap over the bull's back,

(49) Here a charming picture of a boy gathering basketfuls of wild crocus flowers. The Minoan's love of nature comes out very clearly here, as in many scenes of out-of-door life, and in marine pieces where fish, the octopus, and the nautilus, are realistically drawn.

(50) The fresco painter, applying his colour to the wet plaster, had to work quickly and could not afford to make mistakes, because a line once drawn could not be rubbed out or altered in any way. The paintings therefore are impressionistic sketches. The delicacy of Minoan craftsmanship is seen in the statuettes of gold and ivory. Only the best artists would be entrusted with materials so precious, and in these little figures —they average about six inches in height— we have real masterpieces of Cretan art.

This figure of a boy god, carved in ivory, wearing a loin-cloth of beaten gold (probably the cap, now missing, was also of gold), is a superb piece of miniature sculpture. The extremely narrow waist is a concession to convention—the Cretan ideal of beauty insisted on this; but otherwise there is nothing primitive about it.

(51) A second statuette shows again a boy god, but this time one far younger, a chubby child; the golden loin-cloth and diadem which he once wore are missing. He stands on tip-toe, the body slightly bent back, the arms (one is lost) raised as if in adoration. Every detail is exquisitely finished and it is impossible not to recognize the intention of the artist—he figures the god with the physique of a little child, but with a resilience and latent strength that raises him above mere humanity.

(52) Completely human, on the other hand, are the roistering peasants of the "Harvesters' vase," a vase of black stone beautifully carved with a scene of a rustic procession led by a queerly dressed old man and accompanied by a shaven-headed fellow who shakes a systrum or rattle, while his followers bellow open-mouthed. Here is pure naturalism, with as pice of humour, depicting a "Harvest Home" as it was observed in every Cretan village.

(53, 54) And for naturalism again we may turn to the reliefs in coloured faience found in one of the treasuries of the palace; the goat with her kids is remarkable not only for the perfection of its modelling in low relief and the skill of the grouping, but also for the sympathy with which the artist has observed nature. One may compare the gentleness of this scene with the equally truthful (but more schematized) representations of the "bull game," the tradition of which lies behind the legend of the Minotaur. Here, on a carved stone vessel, the acrobat makes his dangerous leap over a bull which is the very epitome of fury and strength.

64

Ur of the Chaldees

The most important result obtained from the excavations at Ur was that the dated history of Mesopotamia was carried back for half a millennium and the culture of a period hitherto quite unknown was illustrated by the astonishing richness of the royal tombs. Since that time we have learned, both from Ur and from many other excavated sites, a great deal about yet earlier epochs; but although the sequence of prehistoric cultures is clearly established, the actual dates of them are still a matter of dispute, whereas the First Dynasty of Ur, formerly assumed to be but a mythological invention, has entered into history proper. Our written record now begins about 2600 B.C.; it marks a late phase in man's occupation of the river land, well down in the "Early Dynastic" period, which is the fourth of the periods into which archaeology divides Mesopotamian pre-history, a phase, too, in which Sumerian civilization had already reached its zenith; but for that very reason it is most precious—we can date with accuracy treasures of art which otherwise would have left us bewildered and at a loss.

In 1919, Dr. Hall, working on a little site called Tell al 'Ubaid, an outlying suburb of Ur, brought to light a number of remarkable bronze reliefs unlike anything previously known. In 1923–24, continuing his work, we found more objects and, in addition, the inscribed foundation stone of the temple, which bore the name of a king of the hitherto discredited First Dynasty of Ur and so dated for us the entire collection; we now had proof that that dynasty was historical, and the decoration of the building bore witness to the accomplished art of its time.

Later on, we excavated the Royal Cemetery at Ur, finding there a wealth of objects in gold and silver and semi-precious stone such as had seldom rewarded the archaeologist; and here again our treasures acquired value as historical documents through the fact that they could be assigned to a dated period. Over the sloping surface of the ground into which the tombs had been dug there spread a layer of rubbish, broken mud bricks and potsherds, a compact and uniform stratum representing a building or buildings which had stood at the top of the slope and had been deliberately destroyed. Many of the pots had been stoppered with clay, and the clay stoppers bore the impressions of seals, among them the seals of Mes-an-ni-pad-da, the first king of the First Dynasty of Ur, whose name we had already recovered from the temple at al 'Ubaid, and of his wife Nin-tur-nin; and with these we found the actual lapis lazuli seal of Nin-tur-nin herself; the rubbish-stratum, therefore, was accurately dated, and anything that lay below it was necessarily as old as or older than the First Dynasty.

What lay below were the tombs of sixteen kings and queens, and the graves of many hundreds of their subjects. There was no mistaking the difference between them. Ordinary men and women might be buried in coffins of terra-cotta, wood, or wickerwork, or simply wrapped in reed matting; but in every case each lay apart, at the bottom of a grave-shaft dug specially for each, and although the rich man might have with him a wealth of offerings in precious metal and the poor man no more than one or two clay vessels, these were just the personal offerings which natural piety would dedicate according to the man's degree in life. But what I classified as "Royal Tombs" were altogether different. The simple grave-shaft became a spacious pit at the bottom of which a tomb-chamber, or even a "house" containing several chambers, was built with stone and brick; in this was placed the royal body accompanied by one or more personal attendants, and the door of the chamber was blocked with brick or stone. Then, in the pit outside, we would find the bodies of the courtiers and servants of the dead ruler—women in their court finery with head-dresses of gold and carnelian and lapis lazuli, officers whose golden weapons witnessed to their high rank, musicians with their lyres and silver flutes, soldiers of the guard, and the royal chariot with its span of asses or oxen. Nor was this all. When the crowd in the pit had drunk their cupful of narcotic and had disposed themselves to sleep and the earth was flung back above them, the ceremony was not ended. When the filling had reached a certain point it was stamped flat, and on the floor so made a funeral feast was held and a fresh victim ceremoniously buried, and more earth put in, and this was repeated at intervals until the pit was filled, perhaps for a chapel to be erected above it.

I had no doubt that these were the tombs of kings and queens who ruled over the city-state of Ur just before the First Dynasty, when Mes-an-ni-pad-da established himself as overlord of all Sumer (we actually found the seal of one who called himself "Mes-kalam-dug the King"), and I was shocked to learn that my view was disputed. I had relied upon purely archaeological evidence, and it was the value of archaeological evidence that was now called in question.

Scholars urged that these could not be royal tombs because there was no literary text suggesting that a king's obsequies were attended by human sacrifice; no such custom therefore could be attributed to the ancient Sumerians. These could not be kings because their names did not occur in the Sumerian king-lists. On the other hand, the most important religious ceremony of the Sumerian year was the spring festival, when was celebrated the marriage of the god and goddess who assured fertility upon earth; this, with the idea of nature's death in winter and resurrection in the spring might well involve human sacrifice (as it did in some other Middle Eastern lands); the divine couple would be represented by a human bride and bridegroom who would subsequently be put to death, and whereas the traditional bridegroom would be the king himself, for this sacrifice a substitute would be provided and killed in his stead. Consequently, the argument ran, our Ur tombs were not the tombs of kings at all.

My archaeological colleagues supported my view, the literary authorities generally rejected it. They were not accustomed to studying and evaluating purely archaeological evidence, and the fact that such evidence directly opposed their theory at every point counted with them for nothing. Of course, it might be equally true that the archaeologist, biased by his training, stressed his own arguments too hard and unfairly made light of the literary side; in any case, there seemed no hope of agreement, and the *impasse* was a painful one. Then, in 1944, Dr. Kramer published a very ancient cuneiform tablet, now in the University Museum in Philadelphia, which is unique as giving a description of a Sumerian royal funeral. "On the bed of Fate he lies, he rises not," goes the chant; "The standing are not silent, the sitting are not silent, they set up a lament"; for the dead king is not alone but is accompanied by his retinue, "his beloved concubine, his musician, his beloved entertainer, his beloved chief valet, his beloved household, the palace attendants, his beloved caretaker whoever lay with him in that place." Here, unmistakably, we have the custom which is illustrated by what we find in the Royal Tombs, and the agreement of the written word upholds the claim of archaeology to recover historical truth from the witness of the soil.

(55) The impression on a jar stopper of the seal of Mes-an-ni-pad-da, King of Ur.

(56) "A-an-ni-pad-da, King of Ur, son of Mes-an-ni-pad-da, King of Ur, has built this for Ninkharsag his goddess"; this was the text on the little stone foundation tablet from Tell al 'Ubaid which proved the historical reality of the First Dynasty of Ur. The name Mes-an-ni-pad-da appeared as the first king of that Dynasty in the ancient Sumerian king-lists, but because of obvious impossibilities in the early parts of the lists (kings were said to have had reigns of a thousand years and more) scholars had refused to credit the First Dynasty of Ur.

(57) The imprint of the personal seal in lapis lazuli that belonged to Nin-tur-nin, Mes-an-ni-pad-da's wife. These, found in the rubbish-stratum overlying the Royal Cemetery, gave the *terminus ante quem* for the dating of the tombs; the latest of them was necessarily earlier than the king's reign.

(58) A copper relief that decorated the front of the temple at al 'Ubaid illustrated the high level of art and technical skill attained by the Sumerians in the days of the First Dynasty of Ur.

(59) Part of a royal gaming-board. The animal designs on the shell plaques are done by cutting away the background and engraving the details and then filling the hollows with a black paste, or, sometimes, with black and red.

(60) Gold vessels. We can safely assume that only the more skilled craftsmen were entrusted with the precious metal, and because gold does not decay or deteriorate with time, we see here the artist's work perfectly preserved, as when it left his hands. No age or country has produced finer goldsmith's work than this of the Sumerians of about 2700 B.C.

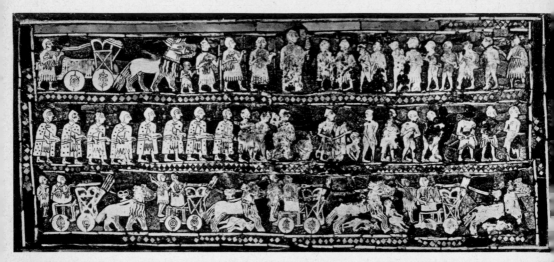

(61, 62) The "Standard of Ur." This mosaic, showing the Sumerian arm engaged in battle, and the Sumerian king celebrating his victory with a banquet, is made of white shell, lapis lazuli, and pink limestone; all the pieces that survived are here preserved in their original order, only slightly disturbed by the pressure of the soil when the bitumen and wood in which they were set had gone to dust. More than any other single object does this picture illustrate the life of the Sumerian people in the early centuries of the third millennium before Christ.

Mohenjo-daro

The Cities of the Indus Valley

In 1856, William Brunton, building the East Indian Railway, carried off from a ruined town in the desert near Harappā millions of bricks to serve as ballast for his line. A few seals and small objects from the site were secured by General Cunningham, Director of the Archaeological Survey, who recognized their novelty and importance, but nothing was done until 1920, when Sir John Marshall started excavations on the plundered mounds. In 1922, a member of the Archaeological Survey, R. D. Banerji, discovered a similar site, Mohenjo-daro, 350 miles away to the west, and there, too, Marshall at once began excavations, which were carried on later by Mackay and again by Mortimer Wheeler.

On both sites the earlier diggings fell far short of scientific standards; the Archaeological Survey of India had no personnel trained in modern methods, stratification was disregarded, and much of historical interest was overlooked; none the less, these first excavations, working at high pressure and covering a vast area of ground, presented to the world a picture which, however impressionistic and in some details incorrect, compelled attention by its very scale, whereas a less spectacular dig might have passed unnoticed. As it was, the Indus Valley civilization was at once, and perforce, recognized as one of the great civilizations of the ancient world. Obviously more exact knowledge of it was needed, and that could be obtained only by modern scientific methods applied to sites which were far from being exhausted.

What then was the picture whose main lines were sketched by the excavations of 1922 onwards?

In the great Sind plains that stretch across Pakistan, plains now for the most part arid wastes, there appeared the ruins of two cities of a type unlike anything previously known. In each there was a strongly walled citadel with processional terraces and monumental gateways; the public buildings in it, all constructed with burnt brick (stone was never used), included, at Mohenjo-daro, a huge bitumen-proofed water-tank surrounded by a cloister, a great cloistered court which was possibly a priestly college, and an eighty-foot-square pillared hall. No temple or royal palace could be identified. Below the citadel lay the town proper, more or less square and about a mile across, divided by wide main streets, planned at right angles, into a series of building blocks measuring each about 1,200 feet by 800 feet; within each block a network of small streets and alleys separated and gave access to the close-set individual houses. The houses of the better class were all solidly built of burnt brick, with blank outer walls facing on the streets, the rooms fronting on an interior courtyard; there were also monotonous rows of identical mean cottages which seem to have been slave-lines. The streets were unpaved, but below them there was an elaborate system of brick drains, arched and provided with manholes, into which emptied drains from the bathrooms of the individual houses; along the streets, too, there were brick bins for rubbish emptied into them from shoots coming though the house walls: it shows a concern for sanitation and hygiene unknown at any other time in India.

The examination of many smaller sites has proved that a uniform civilization prevailed over an area measuring more than 1,000 miles from east to west, from the sea-coast of Baluchistan to the foot of the Simla hills. Mohenjo-daro and Harappā were the capital cities of a great country. And the civilization was of a high order. These people were not only builders. They possessed the art of writing; on innumerable seal stones there are inscriptions in queer pictographic characters which cannot be read today—there is no possible clue to their interpretation. They used copper and bronze and were skilled in casting metal and as goldsmiths. Their artistic achievements, so far as these are illustrated by the objects unearthed, were of no mean order. They were merchants, carrying on an international trade—indeed, without that a high civilization would have been impossible in the Indus valley, where nature provides neither stone nor metal.

But when this remarkable civilization was first brought to light it seemed to bear no relation to anything else in India. It had no beginning—it appears suddenly, fully formed and mature: it had no history, in that throughout its existence (which must have been prolonged, seeing that the Mohenjo-daro buildings have been repaired or rebuilt no less than nine times) there is no sign of change, advance, or decadence: it had an end indeed—a violent end, as was proved by the corpses littering the Mohenjo-daro streets—but with that disaster

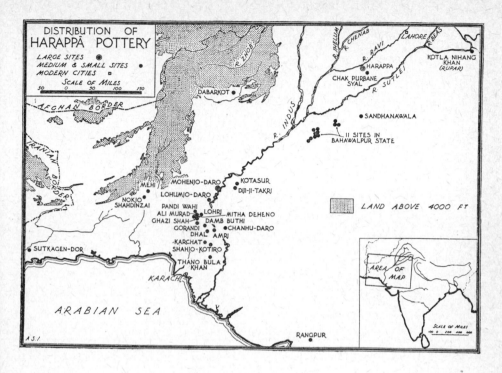

DISTRIBUTION OF
HARAPPĀ POTTERY
LARGE SITES
MEDIUM & SMALL SITES
MODERN CITIES
SCALE OF MILES
50   0   50   100   150

it seemed to disappear, leaving no trace of itself in after ages: and lastly, it had no date; with no literary record and no cultural connections, it could not be placed.

But just as Indian archaeology posed this conundrum, excavations in far-off Mesopotamia gave its solution. First at Kish and Ur, and afterwards at other sites, there were found stone seals of the Mohenjo-daro type, with inscriptions in the strange Indus valley characters. Most of the seals were dated to about the twenty-fourth century B.C.; one could be as much as two hundred years earlier, one came from a grave perhaps as late as 1500 B.C. Here then was the chronological evidence that India had failed to supply; the mysterious civilization had to be dated between, say, 2500 and 1500 B.C., a span of time that would agree with the repeated rebuilding of the cities and with the development of the conventionalized writing: and although we were still unable to explain the genesis of the culture, the date for its end was illuminating.

It must have been about 1500 B.C. that the Aryans, coming from the north-west, invaded India. The earliest Indian legends, enshrined in the great epic, the Rigveda, which had been rejected by scholars as mere poetic rodomontade, describe the conquest and speak of the Aryan god Indra as "the destroyer of ancient castles," who "rends forts as age consumes a garment." The parallel of date and language is too close to be accidental, and we can safely connect the fall of Harappā and Mohenjo-daro with the victories of the Aryans. And now we can see that the older civilization was not so sterile as at first it seemed. Side by side with the Aryan deities of modern Hinduism there are gods of another lineage. Siva himself can be recognized in the three-headed and horned god on a Mohenjo-daro seal; the Mother Goddess was prominent; the *pipal*, the sacred fig tree, was worshiped then as now, and the sacred bull was as familiar to the Indus Valley people as to the Hindu of today; even the Yogi, absorbed in contemplation, is represented in Harappā art.

The excavation of the Indus Valley cities has carried back the record of northern India from the third century to the third millennium B.C., and where before all was a blank we have a new chapter of history which connects with later developments and makes sense of what was legendary and incredible.

(63) Mohenjo-daro; a view of First Street. This gives some idea of the formal layout of the town. Clearly there has been here no chance growth, but the artificial creation of a city in accordance with a prearranged plan. Everything in the Indus Valley civilization tends to give the impression of an autocratic government, beneficent perhaps, but rigid and soulless.

(64) One of the smaller lanes in the city. Close to the house wall was the underground drain, the cover of which has been lifted to show its course; in the wall of the house there is a water-chute for the drainage from the upper floor, ending below in a properly designed "apron" to bring the water clear of the wall foundations.

(65) The great tank in the citadel, with the chambers surrounding it. The use of burnt brick and of bitumen is curiously reminiscent of Mesopotamian building methods and may possibly have been learned from the West.

(66) A main culvert, showing its corbel-vaulted roof. The existence of such a drainage scheme is proof of deliberate town planning by a single authority; it also bears witness to views on hygiene far more advanced than were ever again held by Indian municipal authorities.

(67) How the end came to Mohenjo-daro. Here, in the streets, lie the skeletons of the luckless citizens who were caught by the invading Aryans. There could be no clearer proof of the violent downfall of the Indus Valley civilization.

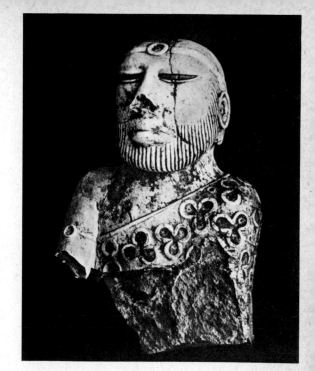

(68) This fragment of a soapstone statuette may show Mesopotamian influence in that the trefoil inlay of the robe is a familiar motive on Sumerian stone vases, etc.; but the head is purely Indian. The eyes, half-closed and looking down and inward to the tip of the nose, suggest the religious exercises of the Yogi.

(69, 70) There is grace, too, in this stylized but lifelike figurine of a girl dancer. Here the material is bronze, and the little statuette illustrates the skill of the metal-caster no less than the genius of the artist.

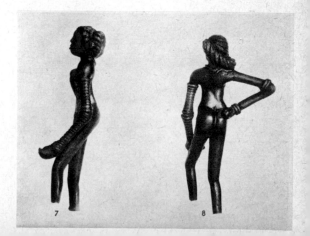

(71) At Mohenjo-daro alone, more than twelve hundred seals were found, but the subjects represented are relatively few; there were stock themes, constantly repeated, which differ in detail but are essentially the same; what makes them individual is the inscription. One can imagine that the inscription gives the name of the seal's owner and that the figure shows the image or the symbol of the god whose protection he invoked. The commonest symbol is the "unicorn"—perhaps an eland or an oryx—but only one horn is represented; it often has a saddle, sometimes a necklace, and generally there is in front of it what may be an incense burner. Certainly it is a sacred beast.

(72, 73) The short-horned bull, shown standing in front of a manger, is also very common. There are no specifically religious objects associated with it, but equally there is none with the splendid humped and long-horned Brahmani bull; perhaps these creatures, sacred in antiquity as they are today, carried their divinity in themselves and had no need of extraneous symbols. The elephant, the tiger, and the rhinoceros occur, but are comparatively rare; all these animals figure in Hindu superstition, if not in the religion proper, and they may have been sacred originally.

(74) Here is the three-faced horned deity seated in the Yogi posture who can scarcely be other than the prototype of Siva. Not all the people of Harappā and Mohenjo-daro were massacred by the Aryans; the enslaved survivors kept to their old faith, and gradually their gods entered the pantheon of the mixed population of India, and are still worshiped.

(75) The seals are normally square and button-shaped, like the small example shown here.

The Tomb of Tutankhamun

No archaeological excavation has ever excited so general and so lasting an interest as that which brought to light the tomb of the Pharaoh Tutankhamun. The tomb's importance was due, first and foremost, to the amazing number of beautiful things which it contained—an unparalleled contribution to the world's treasury of art which the public was right to appreciate.

On the other hand it must be admitted that the discovery added nothing to what was known about the history of Egypt. The tomb yielded no written documents other than the stereotyped funerary inscriptions. The brief reign of this insignificant boy Pharaoh (he was only about eighteen years old when he died) was not marked by any event of note; that he renounced the Aten worship proclaimed by his father-in-law Akhenaton and that under his rule the priests of Amun at Thebes regained their old power were facts already familiar to historians. Of course the tomb, the only Egyptian royal tomb found virtually intact, did illustrate with unsurpassed splendour the ritual of a Pharaoh's burial, but that ritual, too, was already known, from written documents, from wall paintings and reliefs, and from objects surviving in plundered graves; it was indeed satisfactory to have the actual furniture instead of pictures of it, but it taught us nothing new.

What struck the imagination of the world was, in the first place, the dramatic character of the discovery—the long and patient search, a real act of faith, culminating in the discovery of something the like of which had never been found before—the undisturbed body of one of the ancient Egyptian kings. Egypt had always figured as the land of mystery and romance, and here was romance brought to life. In the second place there was the sensational prodigality of the treasures which today fill room after room of the Cairo Museum. It was a curiously mixed collection. Side by side with objects of breath-taking beauty there were others exhibiting a quite lamentable taste; on the one hand there was superfine technique, on the other, careless and shoddy workmanship.

But in the excitement of the moment the public could not stop to discriminate but accepted everything alike as marvelous; the name of Tutankhamun, which had hitherto meant little even to the professional Egyptologist, became "familiar as a household word" throughout Europe and America. It can fairly be said that this popular reaction was the main contribution to archaeology made by the famous tomb.

The discoveries made by Rawlinson and Layard in Mesopotamia in the middle of last century had aroused the keenest interest at the time, but the interest was confined to a relatively small circle of people, and it gradually evaporated. Schliemann's excavations at Troy and Mycenae, in the 1870's, appealed in the main to Homeric scholars and to the layman only in proportion as the layman of those days had his education grounded on the Homeric poems. Now for the first time an archaeological excavation became the leading feature of the popular press; for the first time the ordinary newspaper reader had impressed upon him the romantic possibilities of field archaeology and its scientific methods whereby alone such results could be obtained. Digging was not a mere matter of luck. Lord Carnarvon and Howard Carter had worked patiently, year after year, upon a reasoned theory; and when the tomb doors were opened and the heaped treasure lay before them, infinite precautions had to be taken before those fragile objects could be lifted, one by one, and intricate records had to be kept to assure the correct re-creation of what time had corrupted. Moreover, this was not an ephemeral sensation. Work on the tomb perforce went slowly, taking not months but years, but always there were fresh treasures to whet the appetite, and the very fact of the delay emphasized the difference between scientific method and haphazard tomb robbery. By the time the last mystery was revealed and the golden coffin of Tutenkhamun and the gold mask which covered the actual face of his mummy had thrilled a wondering world with their beauty, it had been firmly established that archaeology was a serious branch of historical research with a technique of its own and that its results were valuable and could be of general interest.

That change in the public view was a vital thing. For a long while, archaeology had been discounted as a rich man's hobby, at best a harmless eccentricity; indeed, to anyone who did not know Lord Carnarvon, his own undertaking in the Valley of the Kings might have seemed a case in point; but when first he was allotted a site and five weeks of excavation on a large scale produced one mummy cast, he strongly insisted that the authorities had done rightly and that he could expect nothing better until he had engaged a competent director. Of course, the public was badly out of date; for fifty years the methods of excavation had been growing more and more professional, and Sir Flinders Petrie had turned what had been a hobby into a science, but the facts were known only to the initiated few. Now, thanks to the publicity that attended the Tutankhamun discovery, they became a commonplace. Just at the time when the private patron was doomed to disappear and the field archaeologist who had depended upon him was in danger of finding his occupation gone, the general public realized that archaeology was really their own concern and merited their support. The encouragement given today to archaeological research is in no small degree due to the long-drawn-out thrill with which the world followed the opening of that unique tomb in the Valley of the Kings.

(76) The Valley of the Kings. In this barren valley on the west side of the Nile, opposite Thebes, were buried the Pharaohs of the XVIIIth and XIXth Dynasties, except for the heretic Akhenaton, who had made his tomb at Tell el Amarna, far from the Thebes which he hated. Nearly all had been found—vast underground monuments, plundered of their contents thousands of years ago. Howard Carter was sure that Tutankhamun must have been buried in the traditional valley. For five years he toiled, clearing the side ravine of the thou-sands of tons of limestone chippings which filled it, but in vain; in the sixth year, just as Lord Carnarvon's patience was exhaust-ed, actually in what he had stipulated should be the last week of the dig, the tomb en-trance was found at the mouth of the side *wadi*, close to the well-known gallery tomb of Rameses VI. In the photograph, the en-trance to the Rameses tomb can be seen, and, below it, the low wall built round the open part of the sloped passage cut in the rock leading down to the tomb of Tutan-khamun.

(77) Compared with the tomb of the earlier Pharaohs of the dynasty, that of Tutankhamun was but a beggarly affair, consisting of only four chambers opening one out of another, the walls unadorned by reliefs and the rooms overcrowded in unseemly fashion. Robbers had entered it twice, but had carried off relatively little; but they had left things in a state of wild confusion, and the priests who had to make good the damage and reseal the tomb had merely piled the furniture one thing above another, so as to make room for themselves to move. Here, in the entrance chamber, are heaped together chariots, couches and chests, stools and stone vases, all in disorder; but what a sight for the excavators when the door-blocking was removed!

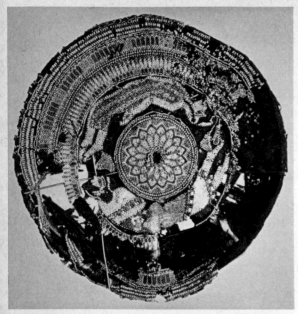

(78) "Until I make thine enemies thy footstool." This is the top of a hassock with a design of foreign enemies prostrate and with their hands bound behind them, the design worked in many-coloured beads stitched on to a linen background. Only the greatest skill and patience on the part of the excavator could have salved so delicate an object.

(79) The gold mask from the royal mummy. Here we have a life-size and obviously a lifelike portrait of the young king. The whole thing is of beaten gold. The head-dress is inlaid with dark blue glass, the necklace with lapislazuli, green felspar, and quartz backed with red pigment to imitate carnelian. More perhaps than in any other Egyptian work of art known to us, the artist here has preserved the individuality of the living man while investing it with the timeless dignity of the divine dead. It formed a fitting culmination to an astonishing record of discovery.

(80) The shrine which contained the viscera of the dead king. It stands six and a half feet high and is made of wood overlaid with gesso and gilded; the free-standing figures of the guardian goddesses were similarly made. Except for the uraeus serpents of the two friezes, which are inlaid with dark blue faience and glass, and for the eyes of the goddesses, which are painted black and white, the whole thing is one rich shimmer of gold, rich and yet beautifully restrained.

It is interesting to note that the goddess figures are stylistically in the Tell el Amarna manner, but as deities of the orthodox religion are alien to the Tell el Amarna repertoire. The shrine must be a transitional work, executed by artists trained in the heretical school but now engaged by a "converted" Pharaoh.

(81) The back panel of the Golden Throne is a masterpiece of art. The ground is a sheet of beaten gold about twenty inches square. Some details, the sun-disc and the hieroglyphs, are in *repoussé* work, but most is in inlay. The flesh of the figures of Tutankhamun and his queen is of red glass, their wigs of blue faience, their robes of silver; the crowns and ribbons and collars of the royal couple, the table with its garlands and the elaborate frame to the whole picture are ablaze with coloured glass, white stone, and dark and light blue faience. Somehow the artist has avoided the effect of garishness which a mere enumeration of the colours might suggest and has made a thing of exquisite beauty.

From the moment that he ascended the throne, an Egyptian Pharaoh was preoccupied with the preparations for his burial. The Golden Throne is in the purest Tell el Amarna style, and the sun-disc with rays ending in human hands is the peculiar symbol of the creed of Akhenaton, which in Tutankhamun's reign became anathema. Clearly it was made in the early days before he became a recusant, but because it was meant for his tomb, not for official use in his lifetime, its heretical quality was overlooked.

Jericho

There have been no less than four "digs" at Jericho in the course of the last ninety years, and it is interesting to see how the more advanced methods and the accumulated archaeological knowledge of today have been able to correct the tentative conclusions put forward by the earlier diggers. To most people, the name of Jericho recalls the story of Joshua and the miraculous capture of the fortified city. The story inevitably influenced the excavators, and it was not surprising that the fallen and shattered town walls which they discovered were regarded as proof of the victory of the Hebrew invaders.

Now it can be shown that those walls were overthrown—probably by the Egyptians—about two centuries before the Israelites crossed the Jordan, and of the town which Joshua burned with fire there survives only part of one small house, everything else having been denuded away by wind and weather in the course of the long centuries during which the site lay deserted. The excavations have not thrown, and never can throw, any light upon the Old Testament story of Joshua, although they illustrate vividly enough the type of Palestinian town that Abraham and the other patriarchs had known hundreds of years before.

What makes the work at Jericho so sensational is something very different. Digging down methodically, stratum by stratum, to the virgin rock fifty feet below the isolated relic of Joshua's day, Miss Kathleen Kenyon has unearthed a walled town of almost incredible antiquity. From the buildings of about 1600 B.C. belonging to the "Middle Bronze Age," which the patriarchs saw, through an "Intermediate" period which can be dated between 1900 and 2300 B.C., she went through at least three stages of the "Early Bronze Age," and found that the earliest of the settlements, flourishing as early as 3100 B.C., was protected by a girdle wall of stone and mud brick, with semicircular towers at intervals along it. Then came the Neolithic period. In the two uppermost strata there were houses built of the bun-shaped mud bricks which were used in Mesopotamia; rather poor houses in which lived people whose tools and weapons were all made of stone—flint knives and chisels and sickle blades, and grindstones of volcanic rock, while their pottery was of the type familiar to us from other Neolithic sites in Syria and Mesopotamia and supposed to date from something like 4500 B.C. Before that time, the mound was inhabited by a more barbarous stock, peasants who seem to have built no houses for themselves but squatted on the forty-five-foot-high hilltop in tents or booths, newcomers who brought with them a type of pottery quite different from that of the later Neolithic house dwellers, a cream-coloured ware with decorative designs in polished red, the earliest pottery to be found at Jericho. For before they came, the inhabitants of Jericho had not reached the level of culture at which man learned to make vessels of baked clay; they had their stone tools and with them chipped and ground bowls of soft stone or cut such out of wood; they would make bottles out of goatskins and platters and mats of woven reeds, but the potter's technique was unknown. None the less, they were not mere savages. They lived in brick-built houses whose walls and floors were covered with cream-coloured or pink plaster which was burnished with polishing stones till it was lustrous and practically waterproof; they surrounded their settlement with a great stone wall built of boulders brought from the mountain-foot half a mile away, a feat which implies an organized and disciplined community; they buried their dead under the house floors but removed the skulls and on them modelled in plaster portraits of the deceased which must have had some religious significance.

The community lived there for a very long time, for as many as nineteen levels could be distinguished, each with its remains of successive buildings, but for how long, and when? That is a question which archaeology proper cannot answer, but two specimens of charcoal from two distinct levels were dated by the "Carbon 14" process (which measures the loss of radioactivity) to about 5850 and about 6250 B.C., both of which dates therefore should fall within the period of the "polished-floor" people. But under the foundations of the earliest polished-floor houses, Miss Kenyon found the ruins of the primitive settlement which the "polished-floor" people had conquered and occupied in their turn. Here, going down to the virgin rock, were houses built of bricks of an entirely different sort from any used in any later age, houses of a beehive-shaped type illustrated for us by a primitive terra-cotta model found on the site, and encircling those houses there was again a massive stone wall, the earliest town wall yet discovered.

The discovery was revolutionary, upsetting all our views of the beginnings of settled life. Hitherto the material evidence for that was afforded by the scanty remains of a few villages, mere clusters of primitive huts, which were optimistically assigned to the fifth millennium B.C., and those told us no more than we might have guessed—that when men began to till the soil instead of merely collecting wild food to supplement what the hunter brought in, they would build huts to shelter themselves, and would naturally congregate where good earth and a supply of water assured easy cultivation. Jericho takes us back to a far earlier date, somewhere in the seventh millennium, and shows us a society organized in fairly large units (there is room within the line of the wall for some three thousand inhabitants) whose members could combine in a communal effort such as was required for the building of a town wall and must needs have recognized some kind of code of social behavior: moreover, Jericho cannot have been unique, for its inhabitants were leagued for common defence against others, neighbours and potential enemies, stronger perhaps and more advanced (as the relics of the "polished-floor" people show they were). To meet their common attack the great wall was no more than was needed.

The excavation of Jericho has rolled back by two or three thousand years the record of man's early progress and has given us a totally unexpected picture of conditions at that momentous stage when he settled down to till the soil and earn his bread by the sweat of his brow.

(82) Close to the spring rises the trench-scarred mound made up of the ruins of many Jerichos, a hillock seventy feet high from the top of which one looks across the oasis where, among palm trees and gardens, lies the modern village. At the foot of the old mound is the house and camp of Miss Kenyon's expedition.

(83) The Jordan Valley. In the deep rift' 1,200 feet below sea level, the River Jordan follows a strangely winding course between swamps covered with willow and tamarisk. The edges of the valley are of dry mud in which nothing grows. Only at one point springs of sweet water irrigate the mud and form a rich oasis. Here, attracted by the possibilities of easy agriculture, men of the Neolithic period, at some time about 7000 B.C., built the first town of Jericho.

(84) Part of a flat-roofed house of the Stone Age, built by people who had not learned even how to make and bake clay pots. But the walls are built of regular bricks, and the wall-faces and the floors are coated with plaster which was coloured and then finely burnished. The ruins date from somewhere around 6000 B.C.

(85) Miss Kenyon started work not on the highest point of the mound, but on its eastern slope, where the upper levels had been weathered away and the first remains encountered dated to between 3000 and 2500 B.C. Here a great cutting was made into the slope, through all the superimposed strata which represent successive phases in the town's history; at the bottom the excavators reached a level resting on virgin rock which could be attributed to something like 7000 B.C. The steps seen in the photograph are the earthcut steps used by the workmen.

(86, 87) But these people have left a more astonishing and intimate record of themselves. Under the polished floors were the graves containing their bodies, but these were generally headless. What they did with their dead was to remove the skulls, strip off skin and flesh and then model over the bones a plaster portrait of the man as he had been in life. These vivid portraits in which the sensitive rendering of the features is enlivened by the shell inlay of the eyes are unique amongst the creations of Neolithic man and rank high in the art of any age.

(88) A deep trench shows the face of the earliest wall. Its builders first cut a moat nearly thirty feet wide and ten feet deep in the solid rock; then, on the inner lip of the moat, they built the wall against a filling of earth and rubble; it still stands to a height of nearly twenty feet.

(89) The houses of the "polished-floor" people were built up against the inner face of a massive town wall of untrimmed boulders. This can be seen in the upper part of the photograph. But below it is another stone wall (a workman is standing on the top) which is the town wall of the oldest Jericho.

(90) The houses of that time were circular, the floors well below the level of the ground outside and approached by flights of steps. The walls (of mud brick) sloped inward, forming a building of beehive shape.

Arikamedu and Brahmagiri

At the beginning of 1939, I was in the Madras Museum, looking at the great collections of prehistoric objects of southern India, and, attracted by a type of pottery quite new to me, I asked the Superintendent if he could tell me its date; his answer was, "no; not within a thousand years." The fact was that nothing at all was known about the archaeology of the south; enthusiastic collectors had amassed objects galore from plundered cemeteries, but no scientific work had been done and no real knowledge acquired. Five years later, in the same museum, Mortimer Wheeler, newly appointed Director of the Archaeological Survey of India, found hidden in a cupboard a few broken potsherds which he could recognize at once as not Indian but Graeco-Roman, remains of amphorae or wine-jars of the first centuries B.C.–A.D. Where had they come from? They had been dug up in excavations conducted by the French at Arikamedu, just south of Pondicherry on the southeast coast, a few years before; Wheeler approached the French authorities and at once received permission to excavate on the same site.

Little was to be found there except broken pottery, but the scientific results were remarkable. Together with more wine-jars from the Mediterranean there appeared fragments of "Arretine" ware, made at Arezzo in northern Italy in the early years of the first century A.D. Some sherds of this ware were stamped with the makers' names, and they occurred in strata which could be clearly distinguished and gave a historical sequence. Arikamedu was thus seen to have been a busy trading port for Levantine merchants trafficking between Greece and Italy and southern India. But in the same levels there were Indian-made vessels, and since the Arretine ware could be dated with tolerable certainty between 20 and 50 A.D., the native wares must be of the same date. A characteristic local type was a dish of fine black pottery with its flat interior decorated with two or three concentric bands of "rouletted" pattern, made with a roller having a serrated edge; they look as if they might be copies of the black-faced rouletted wares which were manufactured in Greece and in Italy alike in the last centuries B.C., and at Arikamedu the earliest examples did in fact antedate the Arretine. Another and more definitely Indian ware was the "black and red" or "black and grey"; this takes the form of bowls of which the interior and the outside rim are black, while the rest of the outer surface is either red or grey, according to the character of the kiln in which they were fired, i.e., an oxidizing or a reducing kiln; there were also great quantities of vessels of various forms, grey wares or red wares painted with haematite or covered with a bright red slip, which were less distinctive in fabric but gave a wide range of shapes, all contemporary, and invaluable for purposes of comparison. For the first time it was possible to date—and to date within the first half of the first century A.D.—a large and varied group of pottery which had been undateable hitherto; and from the bottom levels of the site, just below the Arretine, there came fragments of decorated pots, with painted or incised or punctured ornament, which could safely be assigned to the first, or to the first and second centuries B.C. One short dig, properly conducted, had laid the foundations of a chronology of the prehistoric cultures of southern India.

The next step was to test the value of the results obtained from Arikamedu.

One of the outstanding puzzles of Indian archaeology was the dating of the megalithic tombs of the South. In many places, from Mysore to Hyderabad, there were known enormous cemeteries marked by mounds and stone circles; very many of them had been opened and plundered. All the graves were of one type. A hole was dug down in the soil, and in it was constructed a cist or chamber built of huge slabs of stone, one for each side, one for the floor and one for the roof; the chamber would measure about seven feet by four, and the slab at one end had, high up in it, a circular "porthole" through which offerings could be made; a sloped passage led down to this opening, but after the interment a flat slab placed against the first closed it, and the passage would be walled up or filled with earth. The space between the walls of the chamber and the sides of the pit in which it stood was packed with stone rubble, and this might be capped by a dry-stone wall inclined inward over heaped earth to form a revetted mound, or large boulders would be set in a circle round the pit to contain an earth tumulus. Now almost exactly similar tombs, provided with the same curious porthole stone, are found in the Caucasus area, in Palestine, in Sardinia and Spain, in northwest Europe and in the British Isles. It was natural to think that there must be some connection; and since the British megalithic tombs date to something like 2000 B.C., some authorities were inclined to attribute an almost equal antiquity to the South Indian examples; it was true that iron objects had been forthcoming from some of these, whereas iron reached Britain only about 500 B.C.; but when iron came to South India there was no saying.

The unscientific diggings of the past had brought to light on a few inland sites pottery like that found at Arikamedu; one of them, Brahmagiri, had both megalithic tombs and a town site where there had been picked up, in addition, polished stone axes, chipped flints and painted pottery. In 1947, Mortimer Wheeler started work at Brahmagiri. He cleared a number of tombs containing pottery vessels and iron objects, and in the occupation area he was able, by a most elaborate study of the strata, to establish a succession of three distinct cultures. The middle culture belonged to the people who made and were buried in the megalithic tombs, as was proved by the identity of the pottery vessels. This culture overlapped with and was followed by another, which included the rouletted ware that had been dated by Arikamedu to the first century A.D. Below the culture of the megalithic tomb builders there comes a Stone Age culture divided by its stratification and its character into two phases; of these the lower, and older, resting on native soil, is the more primitive; in the upper there do occur one or two examples of copper instruments, but stone is still the normal material; the pottery is hand-made and is often painted. The evidence of Brahmagiri and of another site, Chandravalli, also excavated by Mortimer Wheeler, suggests a date of about 200 B.C. for the arrival there of a new stock, people who made their pottery on the potter's

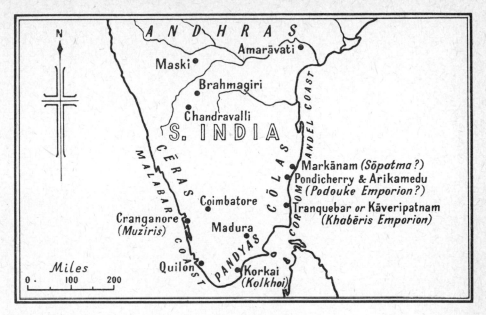

(91) Principal places mentioned in the Arikamedu Report.

wheel, had iron tools and weapons, and buried their dead in megalithic tombs; but since the stratification shows an overlap, not a mere replacement, the occupation was continuous, and we can safely conclude that in southern India the Stone Age continued until about 200 B.C. The length of time that must be assumed for the megalithic culture is not very long and the evidence of the three sites agrees that it was replaced somewhere about the middle of the first century A.D. by what is called the "Āndhra" culture; this is the culture of a people who had painted pottery, made on the wheel, as well as the rouletted ware inherited from the megalithic past, and who were sophisticated enough to use not only metal coins of their own, but also silver coins of the Emperors Augustus and Tiberius, brought to India by Roman trade. This Āndhra culture lasted into the third century A.D.

The outcome of it all is that the archaeology of the early periods of southern India has been put upon a firm chronological basis; problems still remain, of course, but thanks to these excavations, small in scale but conducted on true scientific methods, the main outlines have been established, and the museum collections which before were without meaning have become valuable illustrations of known history.

(92) From the low cliff face of the river's bank there project tattered ends of brick walls; but the plunderers' work has been very thorough and only the foundation courses remain, and those only in disconnected patches.

(93) Along the river's edge, Mortimer Wheeler dug a long trench divided into squares of equal size by narrow partitions of unexcavated soil. Along the top of the trench and on each side of each square, pegs driven into the surface soil gave the horizontal measurements.

(94) As the work went down, markers were fixed against the walls of the trench to give the vertical measurements. In this way it was an easy task to put on record the exact spot and level at which each object was found. The actual ruins, mere fragments of broken brickwork, could tell one relatively little, and for information the excavators had to rely upon objects—and here the "objects" were nothing more exciting than loose sherds of pottery.

(95) But if real historical information was to be got from the potsherds, every one of them had to be carefully recorded. On the flat ground near the dig a grid was marked out in squares numbered to correspond with the horizontal divisions of the trench and the vertical levels in it; the potsherds from each section of the trench's area and from each stratum were piled in the numbered grid squares to be examined and analyzed at leisure. In this way, the excavator could get an accurate picture of the contents of each successive stratum and mark the changes of the pottery in use in the different phases of the town's history.

(96) A megalithic tomb at Brahmagiri after excavation. In the centre can be seen the rectangular chamber containing the bones and offerings, with its porthole blocked by a slab set against it from the outside; round the cist is the stone packing and round that again, but at ground level, is the ring of boulders which originally contained the foot of the earth mound.

(97) The base of an imported Arretine plate bearing the potter's stamp ATTI (reversed). Publius Attius was running a factory at Arezzo (or perhaps at Pozzuoli, near Naples) between 11 B.C. and 16 A.D.

(98, 99) Left: Examples of rouletted ware from Brahmagiri.

Right: Painted pottery of the Andhra culture from Brahmagiri.

Ras Shamra-Ugarit

An accidental discovery made by a Syrian peasant drew attention to a couple of mounds at Ras Shamra on the Syrian coast just north of Latakiya, and the scientific excavation of the site which started in 1929 went on for year after year with never-failing success. By his meticulously careful method and his brilliant interpretation of evidence, Dr. Claude Schaeffer has worked out a historical sequence of pottery, bronzes, etc., covering some 2000 years, which has put all his fellow archaeologists in his debt; but of the many discoveries of more general interest two stand out most prominently. The first of these is the connection of Ugarit (which was the ancient name of the town) with the Aegean world; the second was the light thrown by written records on the history and religion of early Syria.

Ugarit was a city and harbour of the Phoenicians, the northernmost of the Phoenician towns strung out along the Syrian coast. Tyre and Sidon, the best-known by name, today lie beneath the waters of the Mediterranean; Byblos has been excavated and has yielded remarkable treasures—splendid gold-work, alabaster vases inscribed with the names of Egyptian Pharaohs, the coffin of a local king, Ahiram, bearing one of the earliest known Phoenician texts, but on the whole its contribution to history has not been very great; of Arvad, only the great sea-wall remains ("Where are the gods of Arvad?" boasted the Assyrian king in his message to Hezekiah of Jerusalem) and of Amathus, apart from its monumental tombs, hardly anything is known; Ugarit was the least known of all, but today its importance is paramount.

Fragments of Mycenaean pottery found at Tyre, Sidon, and Byblos had led many of us to suspect that it was under the influence of the Greek-speaking Mycenaean seafarers that the Phoenicians of the Syrian littoral who had hitherto been content with a mere coastwise traffic, shipping the cedarwood of Lebanon and the stuffs dyed with Tyrian purple to Egypt, suddenly began to venture far afield, establishing trading posts at Marseilles in southern France, on the Spanish coast, and at Carthage. It was only a suspicion, quite un-proven. But now Dr. Schaeffer has found at Ugarit vases of the delicate eggshell ware of Knossos, proving that the Phoenician city was in touch with Minoan Crete as early as the nineteenth century B.C.; and after 1400 B.C., by which time the Mycenaeans had over-run Crete and wiped out the dynasty of Minos, Ugarit becomes almost a Mycenaean colony. The city proper is girt with cyclopean stone walls pierced by vaulted sally-ports—walls exactly like those of Tiryns in the Greek Peloponnese; and in the harbour town attached to it, the wealthy merchants lie buried beneath the floors of their houses in vaulted stone tombs that recall earlier tombs in Crete, Cyprus, and Mycenae, and the objects deposited with the dead are mainly Mycenaean. Obviously there was in the town a colony of Mycenaean Greeks who were among the leaders of the local society, the chief merchants in what was a very prosperous commer-cial community and, we may be sure, the prime movers in the Phoenician expansion which was to spread over the Mediterranean that hybrid civilization in which the arts of Egypt, Mesopotamia, Anatolia, and the Aegean all played a part. This is not merely a matter of professional interest to the archaeologist; it is a vital fact for the historian who would trace the development of the modern world from its roots in antiquity.

Similarly, Dr. Schaeffer's second great discovery, which no one could have foreseen, might at first sight seem so narrowly specialized as to appeal only to the scientific Orientalist, but in fact proves to be of absorbing interest to a far wider circle.

In a large thirteenth-century building which he had good reason to describe as the house of the High Priest of Ugarit—the High Priest, probably, of the god Dagon—Dr. Schaeffer found a great hoard of inscribed clay tablets, many of them bearing religious texts; and later, in the royal palace, he found the State archives filled with tablets (still arranged in geographical groups) containing the correspondence between the king of Ugarit and the Hittite kings and their allies, the rulers of Carchemish and of the Amorites. The importance of these last for the political history of the period can hardly be exaggerated, but it is the religious texts that strike us most intimately.

We have here long mythological poems which, for the first time, give us an insight into the religious beliefs of the early Canaanites, with whom the Hebrew people were so closely connected; because of that connection they can throw light upon the primitive faith of the Hebrews. Sometimes they explain a difficulty or an abstruse allusion in the Old Testament. Thus, when we read in the 82nd Psalm that Jehovah, presiding over the assembly of the gods, says to them,

> I have said "Ye are gods,
> Ye are all children of the Most High,
> Yet shall ye die like men
> And fall as one of the princes"

we may well be puzzled at what seems a contradiction. But the meaning becomes clear when we learn from the Ugarit hymns that 'the Most High' does not apply to Jehovah, but is the regular alternative name for 'Elyon, who was the chief god of the Phoenician pantheon and the father of all the other gods whose downfall is foretold in the Psalm. Sometimes the connection is clearly there, but the meaning is difficult to unravel. In the Phoenician legend about the hero Kereth (some details of which are curiously like the Biblical story of Gideon), Kereth, who is king in the Negeb, south of Palestine, is bidden by "El," his god, to drive Terah out of Palestine. We who know Terah as the father of Abraham may well be puzzled, and still more so when we read that amongst Terah's followers was the tribe of Zabulon, while the tribe of Asher ranged itself on the side of Kereth. It is too early as yet to assess the full bearing of these ancient texts upon the study of the Old Testament, but that study will be immensely enlightened by the knowledge of the beliefs of Israel's neighbours and forerunners which has come to us, so unexpectedly, from the priestly library at Ugarit.

(100) An air photograph shows the two mounds excavated by Dr. Schaeffer. On an inhospitable coast, where harbours are rare, the shallow bay with its beach of white sand that accounts for its modern name, "The White Harbour," afforded a protected anchorage for the little ships of antiquity.

Almost on the beach rises the smaller mound which represents the harbour town where the Mycenaean merchants did their business and built their rich houses. A little inland, the larger mound conceals the ruins of the walled city wherein lay the king's palace, the temples, and the house of the high priest.

(101) From a stone-revetted *glacis*—a feature of astonishing military architecture learned from the Anatolians—rose the massive city wall; through it runs a vaulted sally-port with right-angled turns to make it more easily defensible. There were similar sally-ports in the wall of the Hittite capital at Bogazköy; but what interests us here is the close resemblance to the Mycenaean walls of Tiryns, on the Greek mainland.

110

(102, 103) The burial of the dead within the precincts of the house in which they had lived, and their families continued to live, was a common custom in western Asia; in Babylonia it was indeed the general rule. But the actual tombs at Ugarit have little in common with the mud-brick vaults of Babylonia. They are dry-stone buildings of finely dressed and beautifully fitted limestone blocks; stone stairs lead down to the entrance, beside which there may be niches in the walls for offerings; the chambers are paved and vaulted with stone, and a little stone-lined opening above enabled the family to pour libations to the spirits of their ancestors. Such was the wealth and power of the Ugarit merchants that they are finer than any tombs of the sort elsewhere in the Aegean, and in dignity and workmanship are only surpassed by the great domed *tholos* tombs, such as the so-called "Treasury of Atreus" or "The Tomb of Agamemnon" at Mycenae.

(104, 105) Of the objects dedicated in the tombs, the most numerous were painted clay vases such as are shown here. They are the standard types of the Mycenaean world and at Ugarit would be accounted as foreign imports. Their use in the tombs means that the Mycenaean merchants living in the port never ceased to think of themselves as Mycenaeans rather than as Asiatics and wanted to take with them to the next world the products of their homeland, not those of the Phoenicians among whom, for business reasons, they had passed their lives.

(106) The Phoenicians were skilful adapters of other people's creations, and they were quick to find models in Egyptian and Aegean art. They were famous workers in ivory, and we can be sure that this ivory lid was carved by a Phoenician craftsman; but the subject and the style are borrowed from Crete, and the goddess wears the flounced skirt familiar to us through Minoan figures.

(107) A gold bowl, on the other hand, shows the skill with which the Phoenician artist could combine motives and treatment derived from totally different sources; here he has borrowed both from the Aegean and from Egypt, but although the Egyptian influence is by far the stronger the bowl could never have been produced in the Nile valley; it is a magnificent but still a characteristic example of Phoenician work.

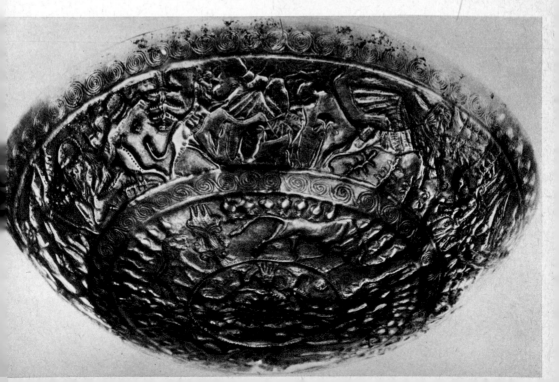

(108) The kings of Ugarit employed "dynastic" cylinder seals of Babylonian type, which were handed down from father to son; this one bears the name of Niqmad II and shows the king standing in the presence of his god *(top)*.

Throughout the Middle East; the diplomatic language was Akkadian, written in the Babylonian cuneiform script. Correspondence would be signed by the impression of the royal seal stamped (or rolled out, if the seal was a cylinder) on the wet clay; the name upon the seal might of course be written not in Akkadian but in the language—and perhaps in the script—of the respective kingdoms.

(109) On a series of tablets dealing with the negotiations for and the terms of a treaty of alliance between the Great King of the Hittites and Niqmad, King of Ugarit, we have the impression of a round stamp seal which bears, in Hittite hieroglyphs, the names of Suppiluliuma of Bogazköy and his queen, Tawananna.

114

(110) Ini-Teshub, King of Carchemish, uses a cylinder seal with bilingual inscription in cuneiform and in hieroglyphs to sign a document fixing the damages to be paid by certain citizens of Ugarit who were responsible for the murder of a foreign merchant, presumably one of his subjects.

(111) Among the tablets found in the high priest's house there were some of an entirely new sort. They were written in ordinary cuneiform signs, but in the Phoenician language, and each cuneiform sign, instead of representing a syllable formed of (generally) two consonants and a vowel, as in Babylonian and Akkadian, was used to designate only the initial consonant of that syllable. Some clever Phoenician scribe of Ugarit, wishing to write in his own language but finding that the Babylonian syllables were ill-suited to his Phoenician words, had invented the principle of the alphabet! Actually his system did not take on, and the later Phoenician alphabet, from which the Greek and our own alphabets are derived, was worked out elsewhere in Syria; but at least we must give to the Ugarit scribe all credit for a genial idea. This is the earliest in date of the alphabetic texts.

(112) And here is one of the religious tablets from the high priest's library giving part of the text of the Legend of Kereth.

115

Serindia I

This is the story not of one excavation but of scores of excavations conducted in the course of the most daring and adventurous raid upon the ancient world that any archaeologist has attempted. Beyond Tibet lies the land of Chinese Turkestan. It is bounded on the south by the wild and untrodden range of the Kun Lun mountains, on the west by the Pamirs, "the Roof of the World," north of it runs another mountain range, the Altai, and to the east it merges into the ill-famed Gobi Desert. Practically the whole of it is an unrelieved waste of gravel and shifting sand-dunes.

Along the foot of the Kun Lun range there are a few oases where "town" life on a small scale becomes possible—the map on page 119 shows Kashgar, Yarkand, Khotan (once the capital of a kingdom), An-hsi and Su-chou; but over a space measuring some 250 miles from north to south and 1,500 from east to west there is barren desert wherein the beds of dried-up rivers, and here and there, perhaps, a few upstanding trunks of trees that withered away centuries ago, accentuate the melancholy of a dead land.

Once, before desiccation had destroyed all life, this was the highway that joined two worlds. Through a land where rivers yet ran and men lived and tilled the soil, the caravans went to and fro between China and the West—India, and Afghanistan, where followers of Alexander the Great had founded the kingdom of Bactria. There are references to this traffic in Chinese literature, but these deal almost entirely with the coming from India to China of the Buddhist faith; there is no record of the social and political history of Turkestan—and yet that history must have been important.

Aurel Stein, of the Indian Civil Service, fulfilled a lifetime's ambition when he explored that unknown land. In two expeditions, the first made in 1900–01, the second in 1906–08, Stein carried out an astonishing archaeological and geographical survey of the country. Himself the only European, accompanied by two or three Moslems of the Indian Survey Department, he crossed and recrossed the Pamir mountains by passes 20,000 feet high; he led his party across the Taklamakan desert from north to south at its widest point, carrying ice on camel back for water, and only by dogged courage and a genius for travel reached his goal just as the last water had been drunk; he marched 10,000 miles on foot or on pony-back; he camped at ancient sites and excavated them when the temperature was twelve degrees below zero and the ink froze in his fountain pen; one of his Indian surveyors became ill and had to be sent home, another lost his sight through snow blindness, and Stein himself, towards the end, lost his toes through frostbite and had to be carried 300 miles across the mountains to get treatment in Tibet; before that he had made and packed and dispatched to the British Museum 100 cases of precious antiquities, while his detailed surveys worked up into ninety-four large-scale maps of a previously uncharted area.

One fascinating discovery was that of the "Old Wall." Everyone has heard of the Great Wall of China, which protected the empire from Mongol attack; now, nearly 200 miles east of the Jade Gate in that famous frontier rampart, Stein found, and traced for 100 miles, another great military wall, running east and west, meant to protect the international trade route against inroads by the ancestors of the Huns. Excavation in the guardhouses produced quantities of official documents proving that the wall was built in the second century B.C., when the emperors of the Han dynasty extended the Chinese Empire to the farthest limits it was ever to reach, and was last occupied about the year 57 B.C.

Behind the shelter of the Old Wall, the now desolate country was strewn with historic remains. On one site after another, Stein excavated the ruins of temples and houses, recovering from the former stucco statues and reliefs and fresco paintings, and from the latter thousands and thousands of written records. The documents, written upon wood, birch-bark, palm-leaf, paper, or silk, were in strangely different scripts and languages; many were in the ancient Indian Brahmi script used by the Kushana rulers of the Punjab; some were in Aramaic, the language and writing of an Iranian people living in Bokhara and Samarkand; many were in Kharoshthi, a script known from coins and inscriptions of northwest India; vast numbers were in Chinese, and not a few in languages still undeciphered; from all these together there could be deduced the outlines at least of Turkestan's political history.

The country was indeed a mixing-pot of nations. At the outset we see the Han emperors safeguarding their control of the Tarim basin; the troops they employed were largely the Indo-Scythian people of Sogdiana, the hereditary enemies of the northern Huns by whom they had been driven from Turkestan. It was from one tribe of those Indo-Scythians that the Kushana kings came, and when they had established themselves in the Punjab, with Taxila for their capital, their influence in Turkestan was strong, and it was thanks to them that the Buddhist religion became that of Turkestan; here, then, far from India, we find some of the oldest examples of Indian writing, while the temple sculptures are in the Graeco-Buddhist style of the Punjab. But here the Indian school comes into contact with the Chinese, and at the same time one can recognize an Iranian influence coming in from Bokhara; things beautiful in themselves are also an object-lesson in the interplay of diverse arts.

About 220 A.D., the Han dynasty fell, and although sometimes a T'ang emperor asserted his authority, the country was left very much to its own devices. In the north, the Turkish tribe of the Uigurs were predominant, and in the south the Tibetans; and about 760 A.D., the latter forcibly seized and held Turkestan for a century, after which the Chinese emperor re-established his suzerainty, only to lose it again when the T'ang dynasty collapsed early in the tenth century. All these peoples and events have left their record in the written documents recovered by Stein from the ruins of the buildings.

But by this time, growing desiccation had led to the abandonment of vast stretches of what had been populous country; agriculture and life in general shrank within the narrow confines of the oases. Still, the great thoroughfare from East to West was used by travellers; Chinese pilgrims visited India, the

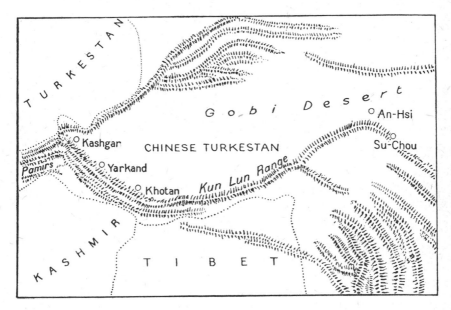

(113) Map showing towns at the foot of the Kun Lun Range

birthplace of the Buddhist faith, and came back with stores of sacred bookes and pictures which might better instruct their co-religionists in China, and late in the thirteenth century, Marco Polo the Venetian passed along it and has left us a fearsome description of "the Desert of Lop"; but traffic was lessening and gradually all touch between China and the West was lost.

(114) The sand-dunes of the Taklamakan desert.

(115) Sand-buried ruins of houses. The houses were built with a timber framework filled in with reeds which were plaster-coated inside and out. When they were deserted and buried by the shifting sands, the lower parts would be well preserved, but the upper parts, exposed to the wind, would lose their plaster and matting and only tattered uprights of the wall timbers would survive. Here is such a ruin, over-shadowed by the gaunt skeletons of two mulberry trees.

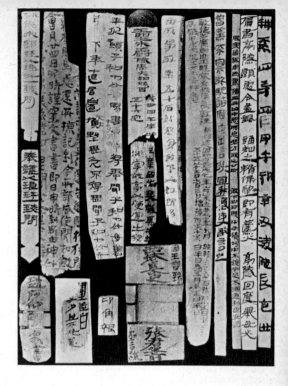

(116) These records (most of those shown in the photograph were found in the guard-houses of the Wall) afford not only accurate dates, but also much detailed information as to the military organization of the defences under "the commander-in-chief of the Western Regions." That his was a difficult task is proved by repeated orders for reducing the rations issued to the troops and for making the local garrisons grow their own cereals and fodder crops; already by 330 A.D. (the latest date), desiccation had set in. The officers were Chinese, the soldiers are called "barbarians," i.e., they were Indo-Scythian mercenaries, but since all their clothes as well as weapons were issued from the army stores they must have ranked as Chinese regulars. It was an isolated post; one document, dated in the sixteenth year of an emperor who had in fact died three years after ascending the throne, shows that for fourteen years all communication with the imperial headquarters might be cut off.

(117) But below the level of the sand there was much to be found. Where the building was a Buddhist shrine, the walls would be lined with stucco reliefs, large parts of which might still be in place. These are, in subject, style, and technique, identical with the reliefs adorning the *stupas* and shrines of the Punjab and were certainly made by Indian craftsmen.

121

(118) In many of the reliefs, and especially in the heads of the figures, the influence of Graeco-Roman art is unmistakable; the shield in the centre is taken directly from the Greek shield of Athena bearing the Gorgon's head.

(119) More remarkable were the frescoes. From a Buddhist shrine at Miran, which was deserted between 250 and 300 A.D,. Stein recovered wall-paintings of which it can be said that they reflect faithfully the cosmopolitan character of ancient Turkestan. At first glance one would think that one was in the Ajanta caves of central India, and indeed the general relation to those world-famous frescoes holds good; but in the fragment here shown, the girl on the left is not Indian at all but might have come from some Persian miniature, the man on the right could be a Roman portrait, and the central *amorino* is also of the classical school.

(120) Another part of the same fresco gives us the explanation. In the lower part, the head of the crowned prince is typically Indian; the youth on the left might be Indian, more probably Levantine, but he wears the Phrygian cap which is the symbol of Mithras the Anatolian god worshipped by Roman troops throughout the Empire. The main scene above is purely Indian an illustration of a known Buddhist legend; but on the hind-quarters of the elephant is a short inscription (written in Kharoshthi!) which says "This fresco is the work of Tita who has received 3 000 pieces of money for it"; in the very heart of Asia a wandering Roman artist Titus was engaged to decorate a Buddhist shrine!

(121) Most of the Kharoshthi documents were written on wooden tablets either long triangular slips which were tied together in paiis or of the ingenious form shown here where the tablet proper is an oblong with a raised border at each end and there is a separate cover-piece or envelope. The upper figure shows the complete tablet, covered, tied, and sealed; the lower shows the tablet with its cover removed, exposing the text.

(122) The cover of a Kharoshthi tablet with clay seal-impressions over the strings which secured it; the seals were classical Roman gems.

Serindia II
The Thousand Buddhas

Among the Chinese pilgrims who ventured on the long journey to the scene of Buddha's life in India there was one whose name is still held in honour. Hiuen-Tsiang made careful notes of the route which he traversed in about 650 A.D., and his book, the *Si-yu-ki*, is familiar to all Chinese officials, while popular legend has added to his authentic story marvellous and miraculous incidents of every sort. Aurel Stein, who followed his track in India and now was tracing his footsteps through the deserts of Turkestan, claimed that the saintly pilgrim was his special patron and in his intercourse with Chinese dignitaries never failed to appeal to the memory of the "great monk of the T'ang dynasty."

At the eastern end of the pilgrim's way there are places where the cliff face above some stream's valley has been honeycombed with cave-temples of Buddha. Perhaps some exhausted traveller settled here on the borders of his homeland and quarried a temple in the rock and by his sanctity induced others to follow his example and start a community of monks. Stein found one such group of shrines in a garden at Ara-tam, shrines ruinous and deserted, and south of T'a-shih, the "Valley of the Myriad Buddhas," a vastly larger group kept in good repair and housing a priestly community; but his great discovery was made in the Caves of the Thousand Buddhas near the Chinese town of Tun-huang. These were not unknown, for they had been visited by a Hungarian expedition as early as 1879, and they were not entirely deserted, for though they were dilapidated and most of the forecourts of the chapels had decayed away, people still flocked there for an annual festival and a few Taoist monks lived there, one at least of whom had been energetic enough to collect money to repair his favourite temple. The real reason for Stein's visit was a rumour that some two years earlier the priest had found a walled-up chapel filled with ancient documents; inquiry on the spot proved the rumour to be true. Accompanied by his Chinese interpreter, Stein paid an official call on the priest and asked to be shown his restored cave-temple; as he passed through the lofty antechapel, all new and lavishly painted, and through the high passage giving access to the main cella, "I could not help," wrote Stein, "glancing to the right where an ugly patch of unplastered brickwork masked the door of the hidden chapel"; the manuscripts were there, but how to see them? and, yet more difficult, acquire any of them? Tact is always a valuable asset for an archaeologist, but here supreme tact was called for.

Amongst the new frescoes that adorned the antechapel was one showing Hiuen-Tsiang, on his return journey from India, with his steed laden with big bundles of manuscripts, miraculously crossing a torrent flood. It was a good omen, and Stein dwelt at length on the subject of his Chinese patron saint; by the time he departed for the night he had clearly made a good impression, and he left his interpreter behind to urge that the priest should let him see at least a sample of the hidden treasures. Late at night the interpreter came to Stein's tent with a bundle of rolls, Chinese versions of some of the Buddhist sacred books; at the end of each was a note stating that those had been brought back from India and translated by Hiuen-Tsiang himself! Here was a miracle, and an omen that could not be disregarded. The ancient pilgrim had brought the books for men's better instruction in the faith, and for more than 1,200 years they had been lost to view and his purposes frustrated; now his faithful follower had arrived on the scene, just after their rediscovery, and his one desire was to have them studied and published abroad for the edification of mankind; manifestly this was Hiuen-Tsiang's doing.

The priest was nervous—what would his patrons in the oasis say if they heard that he was betraying his trust?—but the divine guidance was convincing;

first the interpreter and then Stein himself was permitted to look through the now unblocked doorway of the side chapel. An astonishing sight met his eyes—500 cubic feet of manuscripts, rolls tied in bundles and heaped in layers, without any order, to a height of ten feet, almost filled the room.

The priest began to pull out bundles for their inspection. The first which emerged consisted of thick rolls about a foot high and often ten yards or more long, Chinese translations of Buddhist canonical texts, all showing signs of constant use but all in a marvellous state of preservation; in this arid valley, in a rock-cut cell of which the door had been bricked up and proofed with painted plaster, conditions had been ideal, and although they had been there since the middle of the ninth century, the manuscripts had come to no harm whatsoever. Next came Tibetan rolls, also religious texts, and then others in the ancient Brahmi script; to the old Taoist priest these were far less interesting than the Chinese scriptures, and for what came after that he had no use at all, but for Stein here was the prize of prizes. Opening a large packet done up in a sheet of coloured canvas, he found it full of paintings on thin silk and on linen, temple banners painted with Buddhas or scenes from Buddhist legend, in Indian style, narrow streamers two or three feet long; other bundles contained larger paintings, all on silk, big pictures six feet square with scenes as elaborate as those of the ancient frescoes on the walls of the old grottoes, a veritable treasure of early Oriental art. The priest, anxious to distract attention from his precious Buddhist texts, groped eagerly for such miscellaneous rubbish as these paintings, and almost thrust them upon Stein, together with manuscripts in what for him was unintelligible writing; Stein carefully packed them up and placed them apart for what he diplomatically called "closer examination," which "examination," of course, involved their removal to his own tent. But for the moment he left them where they were. At the day's end he had another long talk with the priest about their common hero and saint who so clearly wished that his collections should be made accessible to Western scholars; by letting them go, he urged, the Taoist would acquire religious merit: that in addition an ample donation would be forthcoming for the benefit of the shrine he had so piously tried to restore to its original glory was a consideration hinted at but not unduly stressed. Late that night the interpreter brought the bundle to the tent, and for seven more nights in succession toiled down in the dark with a heavy load of paintings and manuscripts; when Stein left the

Caves of the Thousand Buddhas he took with him twelve packing-cases full; later he returned for more, and in the end, twenty-four cases of manuscripts and five of pictures and other art treasures from the same one cave reached the British Museum. It was an unparalleled archaeological "scoop."

(123) Each temple originally had a front porch, or antechamber, which in most cases had been destroyed by the weathering of the soft rock. From this a passage led back to the main shrine, a room perhaps as much as forty-five feet square; the whole of its walls and ceiling were plastered and frescoed, and facing the entrance there would be a platform, or an alcove, with a great stucco statue of Buddha and smaller figures of his attendants or worshippers.

(124) The richness of the decoration is shown by this photograph of the interior of one of the shrines in which the T'ang paintings are still preserved. In many instances the frescoes, and still more the statues, had been spoiled by the efforts of pious but inartistic "restorers."

(125) The contents of the bundles which the Taoist priest prized most highly were the Chinese texts dealing with the Buddhist religion, such as are to be seen here. They were of very different characters. Nos. 1, 2, and 3 in the photograph are real manuscripts, hand-written, but whereas No. 1 is the old-fashioned roll, Nos. 2 and 3 are in book form. No. 4 is a little book of ink "rubbings" from inscriptions on stone; Nos. 5 and 6 are Buddhist texts printed from wooden blocks, and each is headed with a wood engraving; the roll, No. 6, is dated to the year 864 A.D.—six hundred years before Caxton printed his first book.

(126) More important in Stein's eyes were the non-Chinese documents in this polyglot collection. Of the texts shown here, No. 1 is written in Sanskrit on palm-leaves; No. 2, a paper roll, is a Manichaean "Confession of Sins" in early Turkish; No. 3 is a book in Runic Turki; Nos. 4 and 6 are Uigur texts in book form; No. 5 in the formal and the cursive type of Central Asian Brahmi writing—the latter on the back of a Chinese manuscript; No. 8 is Sogdian, and No. 9 is Tibetan. Never before had the students of Far Eastern languages had such a wealth of material placed at their disposal.

(127, 128) Two banners of very fine silk gauze painted with figures of Bodhisattvas —incarnations of Buddha. The originals are about two feet long. Although the subjects are taken from India, the home of Buddhism, the treatment is purely Chinese; they have been translated by Chinese artists precisely as the subjects of the Christian Bible were transformed by Italian or Flemish painters.

◀

(129) A large painting on silk (the actual length is 4 feet 6 inches) dated to 864 A.D. The main figures are various incarnations of Buddha; the small figures along the base are portraits of the donors who presented the picture to the temple.

(130) A picture $5\frac{1}{2}$ feet high, hand-embroidered in silk. Buddha is shown between disciples; the tiny figures at the bottom are those of the donors. Scarcely any genuine specimens of Buddhist religious pictures of anything like T'ang date have survived in China or Japan, so that the Caves of the Thousand Buddhas throw an almost entirely new light upon the early history of Far Eastern art.

131

Karatepe
and the Hittite
Hieroglyphs

In the year 1879, Professor Sayce discovered the Hittites. At that time all that was known about them came from casual references in the Old Testament which, with one exception, represented them as merely one of the many insignificant tribes living in Palestine in the time of the Hebrew patriarchs. But a few years before there had been published some inscriptions in queer hieroglyphic characters carved upon stones found in the Syrian town of Hama, the ancient Hamath. Now Sayce pointed out that the same hieroglyphs occurred on monuments in places as far apart as Aleppo and Carchemish in northern Syria, Ivriz, north of the Taurus mountains, Bogazköy, in central Asia Minor, and close to Smyrna, on the Ionian coast; all, he declared, were

Hittite, and their character and their wide dispersion proved that the Hittites had really been at one time a world power, an empire that challenged comparison with Egypt and Babylon, possessed of a peculiar culture and with a system of writing of its own.

Could this strange writing be read? Sayce set himself to the task. He had heard of what might be a "bilingual," a seal inscribed with both Hittite hieroglyphs and Babylonian cuneiform; the seal had disappeared, but at last he found an electrotype copy of it in the British Museum, and by its means he

(131) The Tarkumuwa (Tarkon-Demos) Seal, with which the development of Hittite hieroglyphs start

did identify two or three signs. But the text was too short to be very helpful; much more material was needed if any real progress was to be made. Between 1902 and 1906, the German scholar Messerschmidt published a *corpus* of all the Hittite inscriptions then known, so that scholars might have something to work on. Work they did; but very little came of it.

Meanwhile new light had been thrown upon the Hittite question in general. From Egypt there came the famous Tell el Amarna Letters, clay tablets which were the archives of the Foreign Office of the Pharaoh Akhenaton, 1375-1358 B.C. All of them were written in the cuneiform script and nearly all in the Akkadian (Babylonian) language, which was the language of international diplomacy, and they made it quite clear that the Hittites were at that time a great power whose king ranked himself as equal to Pharaoh; Sayce's much-disputed thesis was emphatically confirmed, and interest in the Hittites grew in proportion.

Among the Tell el Amarna Letters there were two written in cuneiform but in an unknown tongue. In 1893, there were found at Bogazköy, the Hittite capital, fragments of clay tablets also in the cuneiform script and in the same language. Accordingly, a German expedition started to dig at Bogazköy and from the outset turned up vast numbers of cuneiform tablets, mostly in the Akkadian tongue, but many resembling the two from Egypt. Because the cuneiform signs were familiar, the Bogazköy texts could at least be trans-literated, and therefore further progress was possible. In 1915, the Czech scholar Friedrich Hrozny published *The Solution of the Hittite Problem*, the gist of which was that "Hittite is in the main an Indo-European language." There was violent opposition to a thesis which would make this Anatolian people speak a tongue akin to Greek; but Hrozny persevered and other scholars worked on his principles; already in 1919, the Swiss Emil Forrer announced that no less than six Anatolian languages or dialects were represented in the Bogazköy tablets, at least three of which were Indo-European. In the end, thanks to the devoted labours of students in many lands, the Bogazköy texts could be read and translated, and whole new chapters of ancient history were opened. But the cuneiform tablets did nothing to elucidate those hieroglyphic inscriptions which had led Sayce to his "discovery" of the Hittites.

The need became the more crying as more and more hieroglyphic inscriptions turned up. The British Museum expedition to Carchemish, in the three years before the First World War, brought to light almost as many new texts as those listed by Messerschmidt in his *corpus* ten years earlier. But no such thing as a bilingual was forthcoming. It would seem a hopeless task to get sense out of rows of pictographic signs when there was no way of deciding the sound or value of any one sign or even the particular language enshrined in the inscription. None the less scholars did attack the problem. A few signs were distinguished, first, by Sayce, the ideograms for "king," "city," "country," and "god"; then a few place-names were obtained, more or less by guess-work, Carchemish, Hamath and Tyana, and the words "I am." In 1934, Kurt Bittel, digging at Bogazköy, found numerous seal-impressions on clay which, like the famous Tarkondemus seal, were bilingual; thanks to these, some royal names became legible and a few more signs were identified; but again, the seal-texts were too short to be very illuminating. It is indeed immensely to the credit of international scholarship that in time a great deal of valid information had been gathered concerning the character and structure of the language of the hieroglyphic texts; but when it came to translation (and attempts to translate were many) there was no agreement, no credible result. Indeed, the layman could only hope that the translators were all wrong, for it was hard to imagine an intelligent people bothering to carve on imperishable stone such rubbish as the inscriptions were said to contain!

In the spring of 1947, I arrived in Ankara to be told by an excited Director of Museums that Professor Bossert, then on a tour in the south, had just telegraphed to say that he had found, in the mountains east of Adana, a new Hittite site where, in all likelihood, bilingual inscriptions would be forthcoming. Much excited myself, I asked whether it was a little rocky plateau on a mountain-side overlooking a ravine where, among ruined walls, there was a statue of a god or king seated on a lion throne and covered with inscriptions? Dr. Kosay said "Yes, but how on earth could I know?" I had known. In the first war I had had under me a Smyrniote Englishman, Mr. Hadkinson, who had often hunted in the Cilician mountains and once, he told me, had come upon just such a spot. I had never turned his information to account; but now Bossert had heard the same thing from a local schoolmaster and had promptly taken advantage of it; he had climbed up to the plateau; there was the lion throne, there the statue, fallen and broken now; and it was covered with inscriptions.

The inscription was not in Hittite but in Phoenician, which can be read. But as Bossert searched round in the scrub that covered the site he found fragments of basalt bearing Hittite hieroglyphs. The two scripts were both in use here, and so why should there not be a bilingual, an identical text rendered in both scripts alike?

In the autumn of 1947, the Turkish Historical Society financed a proper expedition headed by Bossert and Dr. Bahadir Alkim, an experienced field archaeologist, and in their very first season the great discovery was made. They laid bare the ruins of a fortified hill-town with a royal palace richly decorated with sculptured reliefs; and among these were found three very long Phoenician inscriptions and two versions of a hieroglyphic inscription which could be proved to be a duplicate of the Phoenician. It will be some time before ancient

Hittite can be read as confidently as the cuneiform of Babylonia and the hiero-glyphics of Egypt can be read by the modern scholar; scientific results cannot be perfected in a hurry. But the key has now been found, and archaeology has provided means for the solution of yet another historical mystery.

(132) The wide dispersion of recognizably Hittite monuments can be seen on this map. Today, very many more are known, but those which had been recorded in Sayce's time were fully sufficient to prove the truth of his thesis.

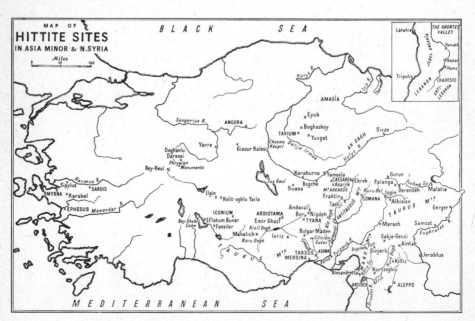

(133) This is one of the inscribed basalt blocks from Hama (Hamath) which first posed the Hittite problem. First seen by Burckhardt in 1822, and first published in 1871 by the Palestine Exploration Fund, the stones were removed to Constantinople by William Wright, a Damascus missionary, in 1872. Wright suggested that they might be Hittite; but so long as they were an isolated local curiosity, the suggestion seemed to have little importance.

(134) It was a very different matter when the mysterious hieroglyphs were found to be not peculiar to Hamath, but widespread through North Syria and Anatolia. Here is a great inscribed slab from Carchemish, and anyone can see that the script here and at Hamath is identical. In these monuments, the characters are carved in relief with a good deal of interior detail, a decorative system well suited to the adornment of a palace or public building.

(135–137) Where the monument was of less importance, a cursive script might be employed; the characters are incised in the flat face of the stone and are considerably simplified; but, essentially, they are the same as those in the relief inscriptions. The hand-copy shows this clearly.

(138) This lion, covered with hieroglyphs was found at Marash, at the foot of the Taurus mountains, at the northernmost limits of what can be called Syria.

(139) This thirty-foot-high relief carved in the rocks of Mt. Sipylus, behind the modern town of Smyrna, was famous even in Greek times—Pausanias asserted that it was the oldest of all the images of the Mother Goddess in Asia Minor. But in the niche, beside the head of the figure, there are hieroglyphs, on the strength of which Sayce could prove its Hittite origin.

(141) Similarly, an inscription beside the head of the chief figure proved the Hittite character of a huge rock carving at Ivriz, just north of the Taurus mountains. Here, the king is shown worshipping the god of agriculture, who holds in one hand clusters of grapes, in the other long-stemmed wheat.

(140) What clinched Sayce's argument was the already famous series of rock carvings at Yasilikaya, where the gods of the Hittite pantheon are shown with their names written alongside each in hieroglyphic characters. Yasilikaya is only two miles from the extensive ruins of Bogazköy whose carved gateways, of which this, the "Lion Gate", is one, marked it as the capital city. If Bogazköy were the centre from which spread the far-flung monuments of Anatolia and North Syria, then, said Sayce, it was surely no exaggeration to speak of a great Hittite Empire.

(142) A row of sculptured slabs. Karatepe was a provincial centre, the residence of a minor ruler, and the artists employed for its decoration were by no means of a high order; they worked in the Hittite tradition, but with indifferent skill. Here, as elsewhere, we find what seems to be a meaningless muddle—slabs juxtaposed, which have no apparent relation to each other, scenes of men and gods and animals jumbled together and making for us no sense at all. Probably they are successive scenes illustrating some legend unknown to us, and would make sense if only we possessed the "book of the words." In our own medieval churches we may see series of carvings illustrating the Old Testament which were carefully chosen to fit the narrative, but could not possibly be interpreted by anyone ignorant of the Bible.

(143) One slab is unique. It shows us a ship on a stormy sea, the sails furled, the crew labouring at the oars, while the captain, standing in the bow, seems to be pouring a libation to the gods, as if praying for help; meanwhile, a man has been thrown overboard among the fishes. It is tempting to think that it is a scene from a legend taken over by the Jews as the Story of Jonah, the more so as local tradition says that Jonah was landed in the Gulf close by, at Jonah's Pillar, just north of Alexandretta.

140

(144) Here, close to the lion corner-stone at the gateway, can be seen part of the great Phoenician inscription which serves as a bilingual. In it, the builder of the palace sings his own praises: "I am Asitawandas, the man of Barikba'al, the servant of Ba'al, whom Awarikus, the King of the Danuna, made great. Ba'al made me to be as the father and mother of the Danuna, and I on my side loved the Danuna. I enlarged the land of the Adana Plain from the rising up of the sun to its setting, and in my days there was every sort of well-being, food to satiety, and all delicacies, *etc., etc.*" Asitawandas was probably the son of Awarikus and reigned about 730 B. C. The same inscription was carved on the statue of the king which Bossert found fallen and broken into many pieces on the occasion of his first visit to the site.

(145) Here, flanking two sculptured reliefs, are big stone slabs covered with inscriptions, the Hittite version of the long Asitawandas text in the Phoenician language. A surprising gact is that in the inscription, the king claims to be descended from Mopsus, who is a hero of *Greek* legend; and his people, the Danuna, can plausibly be identified with the Danaans of Homer, so that we have a link between Greece and Asia. The Karatepe excavations were important in many ways, but the discovery of these parallel texts giving the key to the translation of the Hittite hieroglyphs gives to them a paramount interest.

141

Piedras Negras

In 1899, the traveller Teobart Maler, in the forests of northern Guatemala, came upon a group of ancient Mayan ruins called by the natives Piedras Negras, the Black Stones; in 1930, the Museum of the University of Pennsylvania decided to excavate the site, and for ten years the work was carried on under the direction of Linton Satterthwaite, Jr. The expedition had definite ends in view. Out of the many Maya sites known, Piedras Negras was chosen because the surface remains, already on record, included a long series of dated monuments ranging from the very early up to the latest "Early Empire" times, i. e., from about 300 A.D. to about 800 A.D., and it was hoped that these would serve to date the actual buildings, about which nothing was known; any new objects of art would, of course, be welcome, but the whole purpose of the excavations was to trace the history of Maya architecture.

Around and between the great temple or palace sites whose lofty mounds were the prominent feature of the ruin-field there were numerous small and low mounds which called for explanation. These were excavated, and proved to be platforms on which dwelling-houses had been built, houses with walls of upright posts filled in with wattle and clay, neatly plastered, and with roofs of thatch; for the first time light had been thrown on the domestic architecture of the ancient civilization, which was indeed the same as that of the Yucatan peasant home of today. Later it was found that in very early times the thatched roof was used for temples, too. But such primitive methods of construction were soon abandoned in the case of more important buildings. High up upon the acropolis was a group of "palaces," the walls of which were of rubble masonry while the passages and doorways were roofed with pointed arches of stone, an architectural innovation which the excavators could date to about 652 A.D. There were no less than twelve of these "palaces," of much the same size and type, and they may well have been priestly residences; but in part, at least, they would seem to have been used for certain ceremonies conducted by the priests, for in five of them there were found, in similar rooms, thrones or benches which had originally been richly carved and are exactly like a throne represented on a stone relief, found by the expedition, which illustrates such a ceremony.

For the history of architecture the temples afforded the best evidence, for in the course of centuries they had been modified and rebuilt time after time, so that a succession of styles could be observed and sometimes, with the help of free-standing monuments associated with them, dated with tolerable accuracy. The Great Temple was perhaps the most illuminating.

The earliest building excavated (though this, too, rested on the ruins of a yet earlier structure) stood, not upon a high pyramid, as would have been the case in later times, but on a broad platform about seven feet high, approached by a flight of steps. Set well back from the platform's edge was a great rectangular block of rubble masonry about nine feet high, but itself consisting of two parts, the upper set back slightly as if for the start of a pyramid; it had rounded corners and the walls were relieved by a series of offsets; a great stairway, forty-five feet wide, led up to its flat top. On this wide terrace was a second, but simpler, block of masonry with its central flight of steps, in front of which was a fire-altar, and upon that upper terrace stood the temple proper, a single room, long and shallow with three wide doorways in front and a bench along the back meant, perhaps, for statues or stelae. The roof was either flat or consisted of a peaked wooden frame covered with thatch. The whole building was smoothly faced with stucco, but does not seem to have been decorated.

When the temple fell into disrepair advantage was taken of the fact to make a radical change in its character. The old structure was used simply as a core round and over which the new was built. The basic platform was so reduced as to become unimportant; the lower stage was doubled in height (it was now forty feet high) with four set-backs instead of two so that it looked like a stepped pyramid whose top had been sliced off to make a flat terrace, to which a single great flight of stairs led up form ground level. On the terrace there was presumably a second stage capped by the actual temple; but this has been ruined away.

In the next phase the terrace remained of the same height and its rounded corners and the offsets of its end walls were retained but in front new offsets were provided, flanking the great staircase, and the basic platform of the earliest phase was restored, its front brought forward so as to give it its original importance, and furnished with its own flight of stairs. On the first terrace rose the second stage, only some six feet hight, with its stairway divided into two by a central recess in which was the fire altar. On this second terrace stood the temple, raised on a high plinth, its plan apparently very much like that of the original structure.

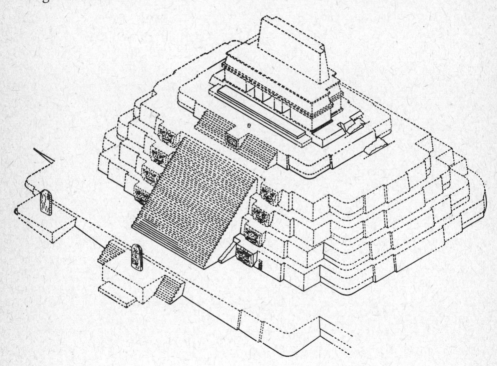

Hitherto all the buildings seem to have been severely plain, but in the next phase we see displayed that love of ornament which is characteristic of the later Maya. The short flight of steps leading to the basic platform is now interrupted by a projecting base on which stands a tall carved stone stela; and a similar stela on its base is added to the platform front beyond the stairway. The recess that had divided the stairs leading to the upper stage is now filled in with a block of masonry, on the face of which was a magnificently carved stone relief. On either side of the main staircase the central offsets of the wall are adorned with enormous stucco masks of gods. The temple itself is remodelled; the three doorways are narrowed, as if to secure privacy, and all the back part is built up as a solid block of masonry to support the carved stone "comb" which is the normal decoration of a late Maya temple roof; because of this, the interior of the temple is very much reduced in size, the old bench for idols is no more than a narrow shelf, and a niche in the back wall now takes the fire-altar,

(146) A reconstructed drawing showing the Great Temple of Piedras Negras in its latest phase. The older and lower terraced building was buried underneath the late work

◀

(147) Restoration drawing of Great Temple II for comparison with page 144 and similar Temple on page 141

removed from its old position on the terrace; with this reduction in span, the architect was able to roof the chamber with a stone vault.

All this description may seem to consist of difficult and almost unintelligible detail quite out of place in a popular book. It has been given here not because it is in itself of general interest but rather to show how complicated is the task of the archaeologist who attempts to evolve the history of Central American architecture. One point is fairly evident; the elaborate stone carvings which first attracted the attention of travellers in the tropic jungles came, for the most part, fairly late in the period covered by the Maya civilization; the latest dated monument at Piedras Negras was worked within 150 years of the time when the site was deserted and its buildings crumbled into ruins. But for the first time we have a series of reconstructions which not only show a succession of styles, but tell us how long each style persisted in fashion; this considerable step forward in our knowledge is due to the association of the building phases with dated stelae and altars.

Most of the carvings on the stones are dates, but those are dates according to the Maya systems of calendrical chronology, and up to the present scholar are not agreed as to how those systems are related to our own: when it was stated above that the pointed stone arch was introduced about 652 A.D., that is in accord with one of several theories of interpretation, and there is a wide margin of error on either side. There is much yet to be done before an absolute chronology of Maya history can be established, but thanks to the painstaking methods of modern excavation, the relative chronology of the buildings is being fixed, and as more inscribed material is amassed, it should become more possible to record their dates in terms of our own calendar. Meanwhile, the recovery of new examples of the arts of this complex and sophisticated civilization enriches our knowledge of man's achievements in the past and teaches us to admire even where we cannot fully understand.

(148) The wooden beams in the temples and priestly "palaces" had often been elaborately carved, as had the lintels above the doorways, but generally these have been torn out for the sake of the timber. A rare "find" at Piedras Negras was a huge panel of carved wood, well preserved, and this photograph shows a detail of it; when one remembers that the craftsman possessed only stone tools, one can but wonder at the quality of his work.

(149) The old Maya cities are lost in the jungle, only the tops of the highest buildings sometimes showing above the trees. The excavator's first task is to strip the growth from the ruins. Here is a temple at Tikal, a site somewhat to the east of Piedras Negras, where the Philadelphia expedition is now engaged. Part of the thick jungle has been cut away, and on the top of a steeply-sloped pyramidal base can be seen the walls of the temple proper, its main door clearly visible. Much of the stucco decoration has fallen from the façade, but above the roof there still remains part of the tall ornamental "comb," whose big-scale carvings dominated the building.

(150) A carved stela found by Teobert Maler in 1899, one of those which drew attention to the Piedras Negras site. It has now been removed to the University Museum in Philadelphia.

(151) A splendid Piedras Negras stela now in Philadelphia.

(152) This little building is the best-preserved Maya structure at Piedras Negras. To the right of the doorway not only are all the walls still standing to their original height, but they even retain the roof, the only roof remaining in place in any building on the site. Before the excavations started, the entrance was hidden by debris; the right-hand window had been enlarged by treasure-hunters who wanted to get inside the building.

(153) This is one of the thrones found in the priestly "palaces"; it is a bench of rough masonry which once was coated with plaster and probably decorated with reliefs. Taken by itself it might well have been regarded as merely a domestic bench or shelf, and the building in which it stood as merely an unusually large house, presumably therefore a priest's house.

(154) But the real character of such "benches" was made evident by the discovery of examples in stone, carved with reliefs, as is the case with this one, now in Philadelphia; it was found in fragments, but was virtually complete. In the openwork panels in the back there are the heads of priests, and the rest of the ornamentation consists of "glyphs", most of which are dates reckoned according to the Maya calendar.

149

(155) The final argument for the sacred nature of the "thrones" was given by this stone relief depicting a religious ceremony. It is perhaps the finest Maya relief yet found, but is terribly damaged, largely because the figures on it were carved for the most part in the round and so broke away more easily.

(156) A restoration by Miss Louise Baker, the best qualified of all archaeological artists, shows the relief as it once was. Seated upon a carved throne is a Maya chief or religious head giving orders to one of the seven dignitaries seated below the dais; on the left are three high officers of state; on the right a group of four attendants, one grown man and three youths. The stone thrones in the Piedras Negras "palaces" were therefore used for ceremonial functions, and the palaces were not merely residential, but included apartments wherein such functions were conducted.

(157) The final stage in the excavation of the Great Temple. On the right, the upper terraces of the later building have been removed to expose the platform and temple walls of the earliest phase; but against the face of the second stage, a big stucco mask belonging to the last phase had been left *in situ*. Of the central staircase the right-hand side has been cleared so as to show the earliest stairs with the lower flight of steps against the front of the basic platform, while to the left of that is seen the middle-phase stairway running up from ground level; of the latest stairway, only a few treads remain at the bottom.

The Frozen Tombs
of Pazyryk

The excavations carried out by the Russian archaeologist Rudenko at Pazyryk, in a little river valley in western Siberia north of the Altai mountain range and about 130 miles south-east of the town of Miisk, were unique as regards the conditions in which the discoveries were made and as regards the character of the objects found; and historically they are of the utmost value. There had never been a settlement at Pazyryk. In the lonely valley there were big mounds marking the burial-place of rulers of a nomad people. When the great heaps of earth and stone had been dug away, the excavators came on rectangular shafts lined with timber and filled with stones; when those had been removed they found, at one end of the shaft, the skeletons of horses, in number from seven to sixteen, which had been pole-axed, and the remains of heavy wooden carts or, in one case, a light four-wheeled chariot; also, there would be a bundle of tall tent poles and with them bronze pots and hemp-seeds. Such offerings lay on a ledge at the north end of a second and deeper rectangular shaft whose sides and roof were of stout planks kept in position by heavy posts; this was the tomb proper. And the tomb was filled with a solid block of ice!

All the tombs had been plundered in antiquity. The original tomb-diggers had worked down deeply enough, probably, to come on soil perpetually frozen, but had not encountered any water. But when the robbers had disturbed the filling of the shaft, the moisture of the upper soil filtered down into the timber-lined chamber and gradually filled it to the brim, and this water froze, out of reach of the summer's sun, and whatever the robbers had left behind was preserved in cold storage until Rudenko opened the tombs. When he came upon the ice, through which he could faintly glimpse objects lying on the chamber floor, normal methods of excavation had to be abandoned; Rudenko simply poured boiling water on the ice, pumped it all out, and the contents of the tomb lay there exposed!

In general, the tomb contained two bodies in coffins of hollowed logs, that of the "king" and that of his wife or favourite concubine. The treasures of gold and silver which had tempted the tomb-robbers had all vanished, but what was left was just that which no archaeologist digging elsewhere than in the rock-cut tombs of Egypt could ever hope to find, for here the ice, as there the dryness of the hermetically-sealed caves, had preserved the most perishable of man's possessions. Carpets, embroideries, and hangings of appliqué felt were found well-night intact, and illustrated in wholly unexpected fashion the culture of the nomads in the fifth century before Christ.

In all respects these tombs answer to the description given by Herodotus of those of the Scythian kings of his time who were buried in a lonely plain on the upper Dnieper (one of them has been found, undisturbed, close to Nikopol in Bulgaria). The bodies were roughly embalmed, as were those of Pazyryk, the king was laid in the lower wood-lined shaft, above the roof of that were put one of his concubines, his horses, his cup-bearer and his cook, and the grave was filled in and a great mound piled up over it; and a year later, fifty of his most faithful followers were strangled and mounted on their dead horses and propped up in a circle round the tumulus—that, of course, may have been done at Pazyryk also, but no trace of such surface sacrifice could survive. Herodotus, too, tells us of the Scythian habit of *hashish* smoking, how they made a tent of three poles covered with felt, and having heated stone white-hot, threw hemp-seed on the stones, and breathing in the dense smoke that rose and filled the tent, started to howl and yell, drunken with the smoke. The tombs of Pazyryk bear witness to just such a rite. Lastly, the grouping of the Pazyryk tombs in a lonely valley is explained by the words which Herodotus puts into the mouth of the Scythian king when he answered the summons to surrender or to fight sent to him by Darius the Persian: "We," he said, "have neither cities nor tilled fields for which, fearing lest you should capture them or lay them waste, we should engage in battle with you. But if you are determined on battle, and that quickly, we have the tombs of our forefathers; come, find them and try to outrage them, and then you shall know whether we will fight for the tombs or will not fight." The Scythian kings were buried in a secret place known only to their tribesmen.

"But," it may be said, "Bulgaria and Western Siberia are 2,500 miles apart: can the parallels between Herodotus' description of the one and the burials found in the other be more than a coincidence?"

From the foot of the Carpathian mountains a vast stretch of open steppe country spreads eastward, following roughly the fiftieth parallel; across southern Russia by way of the Crimean, skirting the Caspian Sea and the Sea of Aral, along the northern edge of the great Altai range and past the shores of Lake Baikal it extends into Mongolia. It was the ideal coutry for nomad peoples who could range far and wide over the grass pastures; and from west to east there were no frontiers for wanderers to observe. Naturally, the tribes whose mounted men and heavy roofed wagons, which were the moving homes of their womenfolk, journeyed ever to fresh pasture-lands, were not all of the same stock; in the West were the Getae and the Tauri, the Agathyrsi and the Neuri (who were werewolves) and the Boudini (who built wooden towns and spoke a different language) and the Geloni (who practised agriculture) and the Sauromates; in the far East were the Mongols. But the nature of the country imposed upon all a common culture, the same manner of life; and while the settled peoples to the south of the steppe lived in a different world and were sharply divided into races and nations alien one to another, the steppe nomads formed a single loose community, so that in a single Pazyryk tomb the man is definitely Mongoloid, while the woman is of Indo-European type. And, whether Scyth or Mongol, they were good fighters in their own way. While they would avoid a pitched battle, as they did when Darius sought to conquer them, when a bad season brought hunger or when growing numbers gave them confidence and the weakness of the other side whetted their greed, they would raid the rich southern lands whose wealth was familiar to them, thanks to the trade they did in horses and in their home-made coloured felts, and come back laden with the spoil; and through fear of such raids, the rulers of the south were ready to pay them "Danegeld," bribes to assure peace; so that by commerce and by bribery and by war the desert wanderers got for themselves the produce of the civilized world. And those treasures passed from hand to hand along the wide corridor of the steppes. There might be little contact between the states and empires of eastern Europe and of Asia; but to some extent, at least, the nomads acted as middlemen, bringing to each some knowledge of the arts of the others. The tumulus graves of the Crimea and the Ukraine are rich in gold objects, jewels of the finest quality made by Greek craftsmen, and in painted clay vases from the workshops of fifth-century Athens; but side by side with these there are bronze and gold ornaments of native manufacture with highly stylized animal figures contorted in fantastic movement, a peculiar art which we can only call "Scythian"; and similar metal objects, and similar designs tattooed on the human body, are found as far east as Pazyryk and exercised a profound influence upon the art of China. At the other end of the corridor, in the Siberian tombs, we have, together with the locally-made felts, carpets imported from Persia and Chinese silks; farther to the north, at Noin in Mongolia, a tomb has been found which contained Chinese stuffs, Scythian stuffs, and Hellenistic stuffs which, even if made in western Asia, yet prove that Greek art, in the later centuries B. C., was brought by the nomads to the very borders of China.

We live in an age of specialization, and the student is apt to limit his research to a single field; we concentrate our attention on one or other of the civilizations which have produced the masterpieces of ancient art, on Greece and Egypt, Mesopotamia and Persia, India and China, and treat these singly, as if their arts had grown up in a vacuum. That is, of course, far from being the case. But even when we have given all due weight to international trade, to diplomatic exchanges, to wars of conquest and to folk-migrations, we should still bear in mind the part played by the nomad peoples of the outskirts; they may not have originated a great deal, but they were a link between the extreme ends of the old world and so helped man's progress. That is the lesson taught by Pazyryk.

(158) On the flat bottom of the main shaft, above the level of the tomb chamber, there were found the bones of the king's horses and the remains either of the heavy wagons which carried the women and children and the household goods when the tribe was on the move, or, as in this case, a light chariot closely resembling the Chinese chariot of the Han period; this is one of the links between Chinese culture and that of the nomads. Here too would be the tall poles of the tent used by the *hashish* smokers.

(159) In the timber-lined pit at the lower level lies the coffin, made of a hollowed log. The ancient tomb-robbers who carried off the treasures of precious metal often tore the dead bodies to pieces so as to get at bracelets and rings and such-like; in this instance there has been unusually little disturbance, though all the treasures had gone.

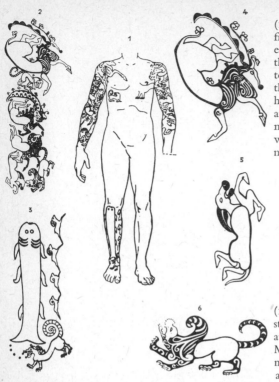

(160) The most astonishing thing was to find the bodies lavishly tattooed; Herodotus expressly states that the Scyths tattooed their bodies, but no-one could have hoped to find Scythian corpses so well preserved that the tattooing was intact. The drawing here shows one such body, and alongside are the detailed patterns; they are in all cases made up of those distorted animal forms which are characteristic of the art of the nomads, from the Crimea to Mongolia.

(161) Here is an example of that animal style on a piece of appliqué felt found not at Pazyryk, but at Noin in the heart of Mongolia; it is paralleled by numerous metal objects from south Russia, and finds an echo in Chinese art.

(162) This splendid carpet, measuring about six feet by six feet and a half, is certainly Persian, as is indeed proved by the dress of the horsemen in the outer border, and the formal patterns of the next border and of the central squares are also Persian; they resemble curiously those on a stone threshold found by Layard at Niniveh, which is carved so as to look like an Oriental rug. Judging by the fineness of its weave (there are 184 knots to the square inch) it may well have come from the royal looms and have been part of the "Danegeld" paid by the Shah as the price of peace on his frontier.

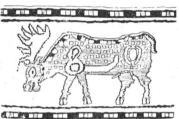

(163) These are some of the motifs on the great carpet, enlarged so as to show the treatment of the animal forms.

(164) The stuffs made by the Scythians themselves were of a very different sort; not woven at all, but of hammered felt. On to the background of natural-coloured wool the women stitched a patchwork design cut out from pieces of felt dyed in different colours, sometimes setting one piece above another. Such appliqué work lent itself best to bold patterns. In this picture of a fabulous beast, the elaborate horns are quite in the Scythian "animal" style, but the wing would seem to have been borrowed from Chinese art.

(165) In the same appliqué technique is this curious scene, the meaning of which is hard to establish. The excavators thought that the seated figure was that of a god or a judge, and that the scene was one of investiture. Mr. R.D. Barnett of the British Museum, however, has aptly cited Herodotus' description of one of the remote Scythian tribes, "the baldheaded Argippaeans who live under trees, act as judges and offer asylum to fugitives"; the horseman here may well be seeking justice or a refuge.

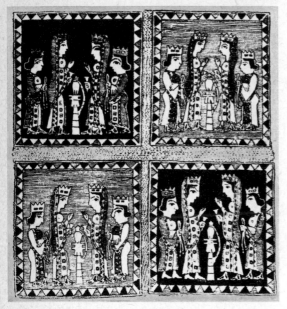

(166) An example of tapestry weave is this fragment, which was used as a saddlecloth. The same scene is repeated on a ground alternately brown or blue, a typically Persian scene of four women (one suspects two major and two minor queens) burning incense over an altar; the Persian analogies, which one finds upon seal-intaglios, agree with the date of about 450 B.C., to which the tomb must be assigned.

(167) Among the objects other than textiles one at least, a bronze mirror, was unmistakably Chinese, but most of them are of native Scythian origin. These woodcarvings all show a parallel to the familiar figures in cast metal which are at home in south Russia and reappear in Chinese art of the Han dynasty.

Sutton Hoo

The excavation of the largest of a group of eleven barrows or funeral mounds at Sutton Hoo, on the east bank of the river Deben and six miles from he seacoast of Sussex, was remarkable in four respects. In the first place, the difficult field-work was admirably done; in the second, it produced the richest treasure known to have been dug up in Britain, the whole tomb-furniture of an early Saxon king who reigned in East Anglia; in the third place it afforded a supreme example of what skilled laboratory work can do in restoring objects that might well have been thought to be beyond all salving; and lastly, it was noteworthy for the generosity of the owner, Mrs. Pretty, in presenting to the nation the most marvellous "find" in the archaeological annals of England.

The mound, which had once been oblong, but had been partly weathered away, was of sand covered with turf and bracken and contained a ship-burial. The ship—no model, but a real sea-going vessel eighty feet long and with a fourteen-foot beam, which had seen service—had no mast or sail, but was driven by thirty-eight oars, an oar being also used as a rudder. It had been hauled up from the river estuary and lowered into a trench dug in the sand to receive it; then the offerings had been put in place in a roofed cabin amidships, and the sand was shovelled back around and over the ship, and when the trench was filled in level with the ground and the vessel hidden, the mound was built up of turves over it. Naturally, the ship's timbers had all perished. What the excavators found in the damp sand was a film of discoloration and—all the iron nails that had fixed ribs and planking still held exactly in position by the packed sand! With infinite care the sand filling was removed and the stained layer exposed, together with the nails; even the size and shape of the cabin could be recovered by noting the sloped lines of discoloration that overlay the clean sand which had filtered into it before its roof collapsed.

All the treasures lay inside the cabin, laid out in order, with the more personal goods, jewellery and weapons, at the west end. But there was no body, and there never had been any; the tomb was a cenotaph. Yet the offerings were no less rich on that account; the excavators had before them such a collection of royal treasures as no British archaeologist had ever dreamed of finding, but the responsibility laid upon them by the condition of the objects must have been frightening. Gold, of course, is imperishable, and there was gold in plenty; but in nearly every case the gold things were ornaments applied to objects made of some different material, and always that material had either vanished completely or was so decayed as to be virtually unrecognizable. The first therefore was to record by photography and by drawings and notes the precise position of each scrap of precious metal and its relation to other pieces, so that the whole object might be reconstructed later on; and this task was admirably carried out. Some of the silver things had perished completely, some had survived—though they did not look like silver. The bronze was badly decayed, and iron yet more so; of wood and leather there remained nothing but an evanescent stain in the sand, or at best a wafer of shrunken substance. Sometimes, as in the case of the purse-cover, the field-notes would suffice as a guide to the restorer; but sometimes the latter's task must have seemed quite impossible. In Dr. Plenderleith's laboratory at the British Museum wonders were done (not for the first time) in what amounted to the re-creation of decayed metal, and the special engagement of Mr. Herbert Maryon resulted in absolute miracles of restoration; what even forty years ago would have been discarded as mere rubbish was by skill and unlimited patience brought back to shape, fitted together and mounted with such success that the Museum could, out of that unpromising material, stage an exhibition of unrivalled splendour and interest. It is no exaggeration to say that the Sutton Hoo treasure is a triumph of laboratory technique unparalleled hitherto.

There can be no doubt that it was a king to whose memory was dedicated this great ship-burial, whose table-ware was all of silver, whose armour was adorned with gold, whose personal jewellery consisted of masterpieces of the goldsmith's art, and whose lovely purse was filled with gold coins to meet his journey's needs. The date of the burial is also certain. The great silver dish (Plate 174) bears the stamps of the Byzantine emperor Anastasius (491–518 A.D.) but it must have been an heirloom already of considerable age; the coins, whose evidence is conclusive, give us a date between 650 and 660 A.D. It therefore follows that the cenotaph celebrates one of the Saxon invaders who had established the kingdom of East Anglia and one who died within that decade.

The first possibility is that this was king Aethelhere, a pagan (and ship-burial is a pagan rite) who came to the throne in 654 and was killed in 655 on the battlefield of Winwaed, in Yorkshire; if his body was not brought back, that would explain why the tomb is but a cenotaph. On the other hand, his brother Aethelwald, who succeeded him, was a Christian, and it may seem unlikely that a Christian would have made, by this elaborate burial rite, a concession to paganism. The other possibility is that we have here a monument to king Anna, Aethelhere's father. Anna was a Christian and is said to have been buried in consecrated ground at Blythburgh, not far from Sutton Hoo; his pagan son who succeeded him respected his father's wishes regarding his funeral, but, not believing in the prospect of a Christian heaven, may have decided to take no risks for the well-being of the old man's soul and so, by the observance of the traditional ritual, gave him at least a chance of reaching Valhalla. It is indeed tempting to believe that the latest and most splendid grave in the royal cemetery was due to the piety of the last pagan king as a protest against the new-fangled faith.

Not the least interesting feature of the tomb furniture is its remarkable diversity. The coins are Merovingian, minted in France. The Anastasius dish is Byzantine, as are also the silver spoons, two of them inscribed respectively "Saul" and "Paul," possibly a baptismal present. The silver bowls with cruciform decoration (there were originally ten of these, but some had perished) come from the Middle East. A large silver bowl, with fluted sides and a classical head embossed in the middle, is Mediterranean, and very likely made in Alexandria; a bronze bowl engraved with animals may also be Egyptian. A hanging bronze bowl decorated with enamelled escutcheons is of a regular Saxon type, but has an added feature which is unique—an upright pedestal in the centre on which revolves a fish of enamelled bronze; it might have been copied from a Syrian original like the "fish-bowls" which were made at Urfa (the ancient Edessa) within living memory. The helmet and the shield, both of which were real armour (they had been damaged and repaired), are Swedish, brought over perhaps by king Anna, perhaps by one of his forebears. The jewellery, on the other hand, is East Anglian. The Jutes of Kent had for long been making exquisite jewels of gold cloisonné work set with garnets, and the technique is that of the Sutton Hoo pieces; but the East Anglian goldsmith had improved on the work of the Kentish school both in technique and in the character of his inlay, for he took over the polychrome glass mosaic which had been used by late Romano-British manufacturers of bronze brooches and combined this with cut garnets for the decoration of his richest jewellery.

We see here a very cosmopolitan civilization, drawing for its luxuries upon the whole world of Europe and the Middle East, a civilization such as few would have suspected to exist in the "Dark Ages" of the seventh century A.D. And we see, too, in the Sutton Hoo jewellery a power of invention and a skill in design, coupled with infinite pains in execution, which, as Mr. Bruce-Mitford has said, suggest that East Anglia made a hitherto unsuspected contribution to that superb development of art which blossomed in Northumberland at the end of the seventh and beginning of the eighth centuries and produced such masterpieces as the illuminations of the Lindisfarne Gospels.

(168) The inside of the ship, looking toward the stern. The excavators have cleared away the sand until they came to the nail-head sand then the stained layer which represented the timbers, the ribs, and the strakes; along the top of either side can be seen the vertical bolts that fastened the thole-bases or rowlocks to the gunwale strake. There is virtually no detail of the construction that is lacking, although the wood has perished.

(169) The great iron boss from the centre of the shield; it is in part overlaid with gilt bronze, and the flat knob is adorned with garnet inlaid in gold.

(170) The shield had been of wood covered with leather. Round the rim were small animals' heads of gilt bronze; above the boss was a figure of a bird and below it a dragon-like monster also of gilt bronze; the vertical strip on the left is an ornamental brace, perhaps intended to balance the two knobs on the right which secured the ends of the arm-strap. It is noteworthy that some of the little animals' heads, and parts of the other figures, had been lost or damaged in antiquity and replaced or repaired (apparently not for battle use, but for appearances' sake at the funeral) with plaster covered with gold leaf.

(171) The back of the shield shows the arm-strap and the iron hand-grip at the back of the shield-boss, the line of it prolonged by a decorative appliqué in gilt bronze; the small fitting at the bottom is a silver-plated ring for hanging the shield up when not in use.

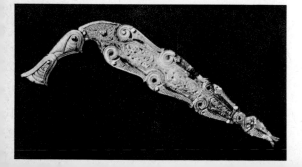

(172) The elaborate character of the shield's decoration is shown by this photograph of the bird figure from below the boss, with the intricate strapwork design on the body, its staring garnet eye, and its curved teeth.

(173) The helmet was reconstructed by Mr. Maryon from many hundreds of little fragments of decayed metal. It was of iron overlaid with other metals. The crest was silverplated and grooved in chevron pattern, the main part was covered with very thin plates of silvered bronze with figures embossed in relief, the square panels held in place by strips of gilt tin. The eyebrows were of bronze inlaid with silver, with garnets inlaid below, and a gilt boar's head at the outer end; the nose and moustache were of gilt bronze; the rest of the visor and the cheek-pieces were covered with thin bronze bearing an interlacing ornament.

(174) The Anastasius Dish. This great silver dish or salver measures 27 inches across. It is Byzantine, made between 491 and 518 A.D., in a style which had gone out of fashion a hundred years before. Not everyone will agree with the specialist's view that its "microscopic and feeble ornament on such a vast dish" is so ill-proportioned that it should be regarded as the work of "a back-street artisan clinging to old formulae"; it is just as likely that the maker chose a small pattern, unobtrusive in itself, because his object was to emphasize the difference between the concentric bands of plain burnished metal and the matt engraved surface. In that he has certainly succeeded.

(175) Two out of the set of ten silver bowls of Middle Eastern make. The cruciform design is probably Christian, and as they are of seventh-century type, they must have been recent acquisitions and were perhaps bought by king Anna for his own use. They measure 9 inches in diameter, they are suitable for table use.

(176) A silver-mounted drinking-horn made from the horn of an Aurochs, a breed of cattle now extinct. The horn itself was decayed and has been replaced by plastic. Since it holds no less than six quarts, it must have been meant for common drinking-bouts when the horn was passed from hand to hand.

For detail see Plate 177.

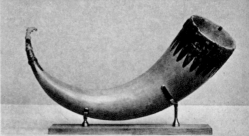

(177) The principal motive of the decoration embossed on the silver mounts of the
drinking-horn is that of snakes—two snakes
inter-twined, or single snakes fantastically
coiled.

(178) This belt-buckle, rather more than
five inches long and weighing nearly a
pound, is of solid gold. The design includes
birds and animals, highly stylized and difficult to distinguish in the involved coils of
the over-all interlacing pattern. In the
middle, black niello filling the hollows emphasized the relief bands; but there is here
none of the cloisonné work which is characteristic of the East Anglian goldsmith's
work. Although it bears some resemblance
to Swedish work, the buckle was probably
made in England.

(179) One of a pair of clasps. It is made in
two pieces which were sewn on to either
side of a garment; in the middle there are
interlocking loops which were brought
together and the pin, attached to one half
of the clasp by a gold chain, was passed
through the loops to fasten them together.
The clasps are of gold inlaid with cut garnets
and polychrome glass mosaic. The designs
at the ends represent four interlinked boars
silhouetted in plate garnets, a Celtic rather
than a Saxon motive.

(180, 181) From the point of view of technique, these little pyramid-shaped ornaments from the warrior's sword-knot are unsurpassed in the whole Teutonic world. They are made of gold and cut garnets, with glass mosaic in their tops. The remarkable thing is that the angles and edges of the pyramids are cut to shape in garnet, instead of being in gold with the stones merely inlaid in the sides; the assembling of these minute pieces was the work of a real master.

(182) Of all the Sutton Hoo treasures, the most gorgeous is the king's purse-lid. The purse itself, in which were thirty-seven gold coins and five other pieces of gold, was probably a leather pouch, the lid being attached to its further edge and fastened by a sliding catch sewn on to the front of the pouch. The lid, 7½ inches long, was of bone or ivory bound with a chain-pattern of gold filigree, and sunk into the bone were bars and bands of garnet and mosaic glass edged with gold to form a border, and, over the whole surface, decorative panels and studs also of gold and garnets and mosaic. At the top are three gold plates which were riveted to a belt or shoulder-strap. Presumably the groups of a man between two animals and of an eagle seizing a duck had some significance which escapes us; but their decorative value is obvious, and the workmanship throughout is magnificent. If only for this wonderful jewel, recovered from the earth and recreated with such skill, the names of Anna and Aethelhere deserve to be held in honour.

Bibliography

NIMRUD

LAYARD, AUSTEN HENRY
Nineveh and Its Remains. London, 1850.

MALLOWAN, M. E. L.
Twenty-five Years of Mesopotamian Discovery.
London: British School of Archaeology in
Iraq, 1957.

BARNETT, R. D.
The Nimrud Ivories in the British Museum.
London, 1957.

WISEMAN, D. J.
"A New Stela of Assur-nasir-pal II," *Iraq*,
vol. XIV, p. 24.

TROY AND MYCENAE

SCHLIEMANN, HEINRICH. *Mycenae: A Narrative
of Researches and Discoveries at Mycenae and
Tiryns.* London: John Murray, 1878.

MAIDEN CASTLE

WHEELER, SIR MORTIMER
Maiden Castle, Dorset (Reports of the Research Committee of the Society of Antiquaries of London, No. XII). Oxford, 1943.

FAYUM AND OXYRHYNCHUS

No proper account of the excavations has
been published. The first volume of the series
Oxyrhynchus Papyri, which as a whole deals
with the texts discovered, contains in its pref-
ace a summary description of the sites, etc.
The *Sayings of Jesus* were published separa-
tely by the Egypt Exploration Society and
Oxford University Press.

ANYANG

Very little has yet been published on the
subject. The best account (although it is not
up to date) is CREEL, H. G. *The Birth of
China.* New York: Frederick Ungar Pub-
lishing Co.

KNOSSOS

EVANS, A. J.
The Palace of Minos. London: Macmillan
& Co., 1921–1936.

PENDLEBURY, J. D. S.
The Archaeology of Crete. London: Methuen
& Co., 1939.
For the decipherment of the script, see
VENTRIS, MICHAEL, and CHADWICK, JOHN,
in the *Journal of Hellenic Studies*, LXIII (1953),
84–103.

UR

WOOLLEY, SIR LEONARD
Excavations at Ur. London: Ernest Benn,
1954.

MOHENJO-DARO

MARSHALL, SIR JOHN
Mohenjo-daro and the Indus Civilisation. London, 1931.

MACKAY, E. J. H.
Further Excavations at Mohenjo-daro. Delhi,
1938.

WHEELER, SIR MORTIMER
has written on Mohenjo-daro in *Ancient India* (Delhi), No. 3 (1947).
These are all official reports; there is no popular book on the subject, but see PIGGOTT, STUART. *Prehistoric India*. London: Penguin Books, 1950, and WHEELER, SIR MORTIMER. *5,000 Years of Pakistan*. London: Johnson Publishers, 1950.

TUTANKHAMUN'S TOMB

CARTER, HOWARD, and MACE, A. C.
The Tomb of Tut-Ankh-Amun. London: Cassell & Co., 1933.

FOX, PENELOPE
Tutankhamun's Treasure. London and New York: Oxford University Press, 1951.

JERICHO

KENYON, KATHLEEN
Digging Up Jericho. London: Ernest Benn, 1957.

ARCHAEOLOGY IN THE HOLY LAND. London: Ernest Benn, 1960

WHEELER, MARGARET
Walls of Jericho. London: Chatto & Windus, 1956.

ARIKAMEDU AND BRAHMAGIRI

WHEELER, SIR MORTIMER
"Arikamedu," *Ancient India*, No. 2 (1946); "Brahmagiri and Chandravalli," *Ancient India*, No. 4 (1948).

UGARIT

There is no English account of the excavations, which are still in progress. Dr. Claude Schaeffer has published very full annual reports in *Syria* from 1929 onward and has dealt with special points of interest in the three volumes of *Ugaritica* that have appeared to date. The political tablets are described in *Ugaritica III*.

SERINDIA I AND II

STEIN, M. AUREL
Sand-buried Ruins of Khotan. London, 1904; *Ruins of Desert Cathay*. London: Macmillan & Co., 1912.

KARATEPE

Field reports have been published in the Turkish journal *Belleten*; a good general account is given in CERAM, C. W. *Narrow Pass, Black Mountain*. London: Sidgwick & Jackson and Victor Gollancz, 1956.

PIEDRAS NEGRAS

There is no proper publication as yet. Short reports have appeared in the *Museum Bulletin* of the University of Pennsylvania.

PAZYRYK

BELL, MAURICE
Druides, Heros, Centaures. Paris: Librairie Plon, 1955, gives a good popular resumé in French.

The Illustrated London News,
July 11, 1953, and February 12, 1955, carried excellent illustrated accounts.

TALBOT RICE, TAMARA
The Scythians. London: Thames and Hudson, 1957.

SUTTON HOO

BRUCE-MITFORD, R. L. S.
The Sutton Hoo Ship Burial. London: British Museum, 1957. This guide to the British Museum collection contains references to other reports and articles as well.

Table of Illustrations

Acknowledgements

Ashmolean Museum, Oxford   46–54
Barnett, R. D.   158–167
Britain-China Friendship Association   34, 35, 37–42
British Museum   1–5,   11,   36,   134–137, 168–182
British Museum, and University Museum, University of Pennsylvania   55–62
British School of Archaeology in Iraq 6–10
British School of Archaeology in Jerusalem 82, 84–90
Centre National de la Recherche Scientifique, Paris   100–112
Department of Archaeology, Government of India   63–75, 91–99, 113–122, 123–130

Egypt Exploration Society, and Oxford University Press   32, 33
Griffith Institute, Ashmolean Museum, Oxford   76–81
Institute of Archaeology, University of London   138–141
Palestine Exploration Society   131, 133
Popper, Paul   83
Sidgwick and Jackson, Ltd.   145
Society of Antiquaries of London, and Institute of Archaeology, University of London   12–21, 22–31
Türk Tarih Kurumu   142–144
University Museum, University of Pennsylvania   146–157
Warner, Ph. L.   43